Revelations

How to Master Your Mind

Sean Walker

Eden Publishing

Sean Walker/Eden Publishing

Revelations—How to Master Your Mind / Sean Walker. -- 1st ed.
ISBN 978-1-7356171-5-2

CONTENTS

INTRODUCTION

What we're seeing today could very well be the fall of the world. A curse struck the Earth destroying people's minds. This revelation, however, is not anything new. Race wars, political battles, power struggles, greed—it's the same as it always been. You can go back a thousand years and see a similar story but through a different lens.

Some of the most epic TV shows and movie storylines are all the same—and the world agrees they are "good." They take you on a journey where the main character has a kingdom. There's poverty, there's power, and there's faith.

We often connect with certain characters that mimic us or others we know in real life. This happens because just like a great movie, our own lives are our best story. We are the director and cast many actors to play many roles we need filled to make the story make sense.

TV showed fictional lives and projected them back to you; they changed the scenery but kept the same plot. That's why we all call many of the same things different and different things the same. We don't have the same vocabulary. We have been taught to relate emotionally where the pain hurts. A healed heart now somehow shattered, and it happened so fast we forgot how the love feels, yet the pain is still present.

A new revelation opens you up in places you didn't even know were closed. A new line of thinking has no boundaries; it has no rules. It's a mystery to one's own understanding and makes you wonder. That is what happened to people. The mind split, causing double vision, a double understanding. What is right was now wrong. What was wrong now became right. These are the issues the world battles with now. We look around and see that everyone was created with different skin, hair, or gender—so that obviously makes us different but what are our points of similarity? How can so many people who are so distinctly different be the same? What makes a human a human? The one thing that connects us as one is our spirit. The spirit is connected to one's mind. The mind allows for all understanding. But from the beginning, the mind, which was once whole, was split into two. We were given instructions to obey that which was against our truest self, our mind; yet we listened anyway because we were given instruction by those who were older or who had claimed to have been where we were before. This mental separation was and is a curse that has been passed down from generation to generation.

While growing up, I was in many ways just like you—an infant, a toddler, a big kid, a teenager, and an adult. Yet, I had no idea what conscious or subconscious was or meant. I had no idea who I truly was at my core. So, much like you, I spent many years of my youth being groomed, taking on patterns—some healthy and many unhealthy—by adults who thought they were teaching me "the way."

We had a personality but everyone started to bestow upon us the identity of what they felt we should be. Be like mom, be like dad, and so on. For many, including me, we rejected the idea that we should be exactly like someone else because we somehow knew it was not our true nature, and we had the courage to speak up and do differently.

From the time you were born, life was set up for you to engage in a battle. That battle was to overcome what you would become because you were not taught about what you already were—a king or queen with the ability to manifest the life of your dreams. You would have to go from ignorance (a lack of knowledge) to learning, from learning to understanding, from understanding to becoming. Understanding who you are is the revelation needed to shift you back to the identity you were born with. You were born a spirit which was do all things, have all things, and be all things.

You were born royalty. But for many, no one ever told us our rightful position in the kingdom. We spent the majority of our lives trying to discover what we already are, searching for our place in the world. We were born at the top—the highest seat available, appointed to us with our name on it. We were born for a mission to do great things, led by our decision to follow the voice—our truest, most authentic self—in our heads. If we can learn to listen to the voice, then we can let it lead us. If we follow the voice, it will allow us to see. If we believe in the voice then we can become the blessing needed to destroy the curse forever. The blessing is that you were born royalty. The highest of value. The most prized position on earth. The greatest seed ever planted. You are planted in the Earth, not on it. You were here to grow big and tall so many could see you through your works of righteousness and the power to believe that the god in you can do all things. You aren't of this world; you are here to be a change in it. You aren't here to judge; you are here to show acceptance. You aren't here to work endlessly for the benefit of someone else; you're here to rule. You are here to show the world the power of love and a sound mind. The higher you go, the more you can see. The more you see, the more you'll realize that there is even more work to be done.

You are god. God is in you. You can do all things that the god in you believes you can do. The power you have comes with great wisdom. This wisdom teaches understanding and restores healing. The god in you will teach you how to be a true servant so you know how to serve your people. It will help you realize that by relying on your own understanding, you may still get it wrong. So, have grace for those still figuring it out. The god within you also has much to learn.

The god within you will allow you to lead without the need to stand in front. The god within you sets standards that hold you accountable to where you are in life so you don't go back to where you came from. The god within you is as powerful as you imagine.

CHAPTER ONE

Surviving Family

There I was sitting on my bed, mulling my life and my future. I was going to graduate high school in a week and with honors, no less. The world should have been my oyster; I should have been excited and swimming in college offers and tantalizing options. It was both empowering and paralyzing.

The truth was I didn't know what I wanted to do with my life; the only thing that made sense was I knew I needed to get away from my family and Williamsburg, Virginia.

It wasn't that I didn't like Williamsburg—it had rich history as one of the first American settlements and a darker side that helped start the slave trade in this country, hard to stomach being that I came from an African-American family—but it was all I knew and I felt there had to be more. I had nothing against my family but things at home had grown a bit toxic over the years.

* * *

I was the middle child but the first born to both of my parents. My mother had two children from a previous relationship, but that never really mattered; as far as we were concerned, we were all just brothers and sisters and didn't know any different. I liked my siblings, but I never really loved that my mom seemed to pay more attention to my two older siblings while my dad paid more attention to my younger sibling, the baby of the family.

My parents did well enough to keep me occupied as a little kid, making sure I went to a good public school, and signing me up for sports to keep me out of trouble. They tried their best to shield me from the parts of life a little person shouldn't experience.

One thing that made family life so difficult was the fact that my parents worked almost all the time to make ends meet, my mother more so than my father. My father felt that work wasn't life, and even though we as a family had barely enough to survive, he was adamant he would never get a second job to supplement his meager full time income. Overall, he was a pretty good guy, but his moods were a little hot and cold, though I found him incredibly compassionate at times; he was just not very motivated.

Growing up, I saw my mother a little more than my dad, mainly because she was a school bus driver and always drove the bus that I would take to school. At home she loved to laugh and joke and play, but her demeanor could switch in a split second. If you crossed her or disobeyed, she could unleash a fiery stream of sass that could make you strongly second guess ever challenging her. Regardless of that, she did her best to make all of her children feel loved and tried hard to keep us focused, disciplined, and away from any negative distractions.

Family life was at its worst when my parents were in the same room together. I'm sure they loved one another to a certain extent, and maybe it looked more "lovey-dovey" when they had first gotten together, but I have a hard time remembering my parents sharing a kind word with one another. As I got older, some of the things they had tried to protect me from were now permeating my inner-being and my psyche, and I didn't know what to do. Even when in my room that I shared with two other siblings—the six of us lived in a three bedroom, one bathroom house, a place bursting at the seams with growing children and big personalities—I could hear them talk loudly and became acutely aware that they weren't being nice to each other. Much of their arguments were centered around money issues and the need for us to live in a bigger and better environment.

Often times those arguments would go on until the wee hours of the next morning. As a young kid I'd have to wake up and go to school, only having slept a few hours because their fights had gotten too loud and vicious. For me, I looked forward to getting up and going to school because I could get out the house and have a little peace during classes and not experience the aggression I felt at home. In middle and high school, I started to notice I was beginning to take on attributes from both of my parents, characteristics that weren't inherently me, but something I learned from both of them. I developed a short fuse just like my dad, and I developed a sassy attitude just like my mom. I could smile and love everyone like my mom but in the same breath could place judgment and complain about everyone like my dad. The more I grew up the more I was aware of my behavior, but I could not understand why and didn't know how to make the internal changes I felt I needed. The way I felt inside didn't match my actions—it was like I had an almost split personality—and it caused me to suffer with some symptoms of anxiety and depression. I began to feel different, isolated a bit, and "less than."

I always knew I was somewhat different because my mom would always tell me so. It made me feel like I was a bad kid or the black sheep of the family, and worse, it made me resent my parents in a big way. I was a pretty well-behaved kid, but my parents treated me differently and were tougher and harder on me and expected more from me than my siblings. Maybe that sentiment was a product of me being their first child together. Their marriage wasn't going well so maybe if they got their firstborn kid to do well in life, they could each salvage some personal pride.

Eventually my parents got what they wished for, more space, but it came at the cost of their marriage which ended while I was a sophomore in high school.

My dad and I moved together to a new place while my mom and three other siblings stayed in the house I had grown up in.

With just me and my dad, it felt like he was a single parent and I started to have more freedom to do different things like get a car and go places and stay out with my friends, much later than I would have ever dared when my parents were still together. I would see my dad daily but some days we never talked, which I just assumed was in normal most families. For me, not speaking to people became very easy. I could just walk by anyone, even if they were a good friend, and I could ignore them because I was minding my business and doing what I had to do just like I was doing at home. My relationship with my mom grew to become very exhausting. She became even more mercurial and would express regret and blame herself for our family splitting up but would then talk bad about my dad and accuse me of taking sides with him, saying that I was treating her like, "the enemy." I didn't want to take sides because I loved them both—it was all so confusing.

I felt like I couldn't rely on my parents or anyone in my family. As my high school career was winding down, I felt like I had no clarity or insight or direction because everything people were telling me seemed to be conflicting versions of the truth based on their current emotional state.

The world to me looked dark and gray. I couldn't understand whether the hurt, pain, and mental suffering was a normal part of life or if something was wrong with me. But I knew I had to get away from this place, Williamsburg, and my family to find out.

* * *

As I sat on my bed, thinking hard on my future, I glanced over at the papers I had gotten the week prior at the U.S. Army recruiter station. One thing that seemed to make sense, at least to get away from my current situation—everyone had always told me to either go to college or go join the military. Either one would give me some direction in life.

I had no money for college, and despite my good grades in school, I hadn't even applied anywhere, bogged down in confusion and fear in regard to the future. But the end of high school was coming, and I had to do something with my life. I couldn't stay put.

So, I decided that the very next day, I would go down to the Army recruiter station and turn in my paperwork, officially becoming a part of the United States Armed Services. I was about to trade one controlling family for a much larger one with shorter haircuts and a propensity to go to a different kind of war, not the kind fought with divorce attorneys and sharp words, but actual guns and bombs. I had barely survived my family of origin; hopefully I would survive my next family as well.

CHAPTER TWO

Life After the Army

The United States Army proved to be a challenging experience. On one hand, I got out of Williamsburg, saw more of the world than I had ever seen before, and met lots of interesting people. On the other hand, I basically traded one group of people controlling me and telling me what to do for another. After four years of serving my country, I came away with tremendous life experience, but I was still in a mental space where I was unsure about a lot of things—trusting in people, my emotional life and the ups and downs of what I was feeling inside that hadn't gone away since high school, and a positive trajectory for my life.

I was still seeking mental clarity and felt I couldn't get that in such a restrictive environment, so when it was time to renew my contract with the U.S. Army, I declined.

Not long after I got out, I found a great job with the Department of Defense. Life was good for a bit. I was able to make a twelve-month salary while working only six months out of the year, with summers and winters off. I met some brilliant people, traveled the world (albeit in a bit more style than when I was in the Army), and had lots of fun.

I was in my early twenties, making more money and working smarter, not harder, than my parents had ever managed to do. It seemed both odd and freeing that I was going against what my parents had always told me ("always work as hard as possible") and having success at it—and at such a young age, no less.

I still had a fun spirit and good heart but sometimes I would have these fiery streaks that would take over. Out of nowhere I would develop something of an, "I don't care; screw the world," kind of attitude, especially if something wasn't going my way. It wasn't a mentality that was easy to shake. I was living life based on what I thought society and my upbringing deemed appropriate, but the feeling of malaise and uncertainty I experienced at the end of high school and throughout my time in the Army started to take over once again. Somehow, I couldn't shake the stories and pain I carried from my youth. There was a constant battle in my mind, between light and darkness, and more often than not it felt like the darkness was winning. There was something missing inside, something I couldn't quite put my finger on.

While working at the Department of Defense, I had a stroke of luck that occurred, a chance encounter that would, in part, change the trajectory of my life.

I met an interesting gentleman from Panama, someone who I ran into several times at a local bar, and a person that soon became a big part of my life. I wasn't looking for new friends at the time, but this guy insisted that we find time to catch up and hang out. Initially I wasn't interested because I had always preferred to have girls as friends. I had found girls to be cooler and to have a much more interesting perspective on life than guys.

At first, I was resistant to this guy from Panama, but he seemed pretty cool after actually getting to talk to him. The second time we held a conversation he told me I needed a haircut (he wasn't wrong), and in no time, this guy became my barber, cutting my hair in the garage of his home.

Around the same time another guy kept popping up randomly, at the bar and a few other places—he happened to be a police officer and one time while getting my hair cut by the Panamanian guy, I saw the cop walking his beat in full uniform. I knew he couldn't have been following me, but it was really strange seeing him in so many places and so often. Growing up, I hadn't heard too many positive stories about cops, more so that they were all bad. But this guy seemed different. Maybe he was actually one of the good guys? Finally, at a bar one evening, we exchanged numbers.

After a couple of weeks, me and this cop started working out together at a local gym. Not long after we became gym buddies, we both made an interesting observation—the trainers at the gym were not doing much of anything for their clients. They were just speaking and getting other people to perform certain actions, but we noticed that what they were asking of their clients wasn't anything really that in depth. Their clients weren't really working hard or even sweating. It was a little strange and I thought if those mediocre personal trainers could do it, then I and even my cop friend could do it too.

For weeks, my new cop friend and I kept going to the gym together and discussing in depth how we could improve upon what we had observed with the personal trainers. We finally decided we could and would have our own "boot camp" as trainers to help people work out more effectively and efficiently while still being challenged to push themselves further than they thought they could.

We didn't know anything about business, or a personal training business in particular, but we felt as if the easier part would be creating the boot camp program while the more difficult part would be marketing the boot camp to potential clients. There would a be learning curve to what we were setting out to do, but we both decided it was worth it. Owning your own business seemed like another way I could work smarter and not harder; again, turning down the erroneous advice I had received from my parents in my youth.

My cop friend, now my business partner, and I began to think on what we would call this business. He kept using all of these Biblical references that I was not aware of at the time.

"Your body is a temple," he said during one of our business brainstorming sessions. "Maybe we should use the word 'temple' as part of the name of our business."

It turned out that this cop was really passionate about his faith and talked a lot about giving his life to Christ. I had never done something like that in my life—religion was a huge priority for my family growing up, but it was forced upon me and I never felt like I was able to make my own choices in regard to faith. It had always seemed odd to me that as passionately religious as my parents claimed to be, neither me nor any of my siblings had ever been baptized. Yet another confusing piece to the puzzle that was my life. As soon as I left home, I swore that I would never attend church again, yet the way this Panamanian guy talked about his faith made me consider that there might have been more to faith and Christ than the way it was presented to me growing up.

Nevertheless, as intrigued as I was, I knew that not everyone would have the same appreciation for using a faith-based reference as part of our branding, so I suggested we keep brainstorming. Soon, I came up with idea that the word "frame" could be used in a similar context as "temple" and he agreed, and thus "Frame Fitness" was born.

The next thing we needed was a slogan or gimmick—something catchy that would bring clients in without costing us a fortune. Depending on where and when you spend your money, a marketing campaign to bring in new customers could prove to be very costly, and neither of us was swimming in money. We decided we were going to try a social media campaign to see if people thought this "boot camp" idea was as good as we did.

While working on our business and trying to learn about what our business would be and what a great social media campaign would consist of, I continued to hear about the positive attributes of Christ and how much faith had changed and augmented the life of my cop friend. I still wasn't sure if I was ready to dedicate my life the way he did, but I knew that something was still missing for me.

The "demons" that had plagued my mind for the past decade or so, would still pop up from time to time, staying longer at certain times than others. I knew I needed to get my mind right and under control because with this new business I was taking on a new level of responsibility, adding it my existing employment and obligations. Maybe faith and Christ could and would eventually calm or eliminate the negativity that permeated my life at times and help me gain answers to life's questions that had me confused for so long. Fortunately, many of the answers I was seeking would come sooner than later.

CHAPTER THREE

Frame Fitness

Starting this new business venture with my cop friend, a fitness boot camp by Frame Fitness, proved to be "touch and go" at the outset. We didn't know what we were doing, and everything was trial and error. The best kind of marketing we had in the beginning was a social media campaign that consisted of each of us with our body in a "frame" filter that said, "Frame Fitness." Luckily, it was enough to get people intrigued.

Word of mouth spread and with our first boot camp we had one hundred people and charged five dollars per person. We figured with a group that big, five dollars was a fair price, especially with gyms charging ten times that amount to work with a single trainer who wasn't doing anything but standing around offering little more than encouraging words.

Me and my partner, my cop friend, were pretty amazed that all of these people were coming out to listen to us talk and demonstrate how they all could improve their fitness regimen. We were just two young guys with no experience and no college degree in this subject. We just had tremendous faith that we could help people in a big way with their fitness.

In the beginning, we bounced around using various open fields in public spaces to host our events. At one point early on, we got a phone call from someone who worked for a city official stating that any open field, because it was a public and not private space, was not available for us to use if we were going to collect money from clients. If money was changing hands, we would have to rent the field—which was incredibly cost prohibitive and would wipe out any profits we would have made. Someone, as hard as it was to believe, must have called the city and reported us; two people who were trying to do good in the community and make a little money at the same time. We had even made sure the fields we used were not commonly used places. It didn't seem fair. It felt like we had gone two steps forward and three steps back.

My partner and I decided we would try another strategy—go to a local high school and see if they would allow us to hold our classes on the premises. The high school that was most convenient to our current clients was on the smaller side but we had to try something to keep our business alive. If we could pull this off, one upside to holding our boot camps at a high school, was that if it rained, we could potentially use whatever indoor space they had available. Luckily it had never rained for any of our previous outdoor events but it was good to prepare for the possibility.

When we approached the high school's administrative staff with our request to use their open spaces and weight room, they were hesitant because no one had ever asked such a thing of them before. They said it was, "highly irregular," but that they would think about it. To sweeten the deal, we offered to train high school staff for free. It was the least we could do and we just wanted to promote positive health.

After only a few days we heard back from one of the assistant principals. He gave us the green light to use their open spaces and the weight room, but only if and when they weren't being used. We obtained an official schedule and made sure we were added to it. My partner and I were both shocked and grateful for our good fortune.

In a matter of weeks we were incredibly popular on campus; staff members either peeking their heads out of their rooms after school to ask us if we needed any help with anything or actually taking the time to attend one of our sessions. Coaches from the school's various sports teams would ask us if it was okay for them and their student athletes to take part in our programming, which, of course, we said "yes" to. Everyone on site was super generous and appreciative of what we were doing. After a month, we were doing boot camp classes, personal training, and athletic training and it was all going on at the school. It was such a smooth process—it was as if this opportunity, bringing fitness to the masses, was reserved for us.

After a full year of being at the high school every day, knowing how unbelievable it was that we got access to such an amazing and accommodating facility, we came to realize that we really needed to get our own space. As nice as everyone at the high school was, we knew we were at the mercy of their good graces and that at any point we could lose access to the high school. We did not want to disappoint all of our clients nor did we want to discontinue what was proving to be an incredibly easy way of making money.

We eventually decided to open up a storefront location. We couldn't afford a big open space in a prime location, so we took over the lease of a commercial real estate building at the outskirts of town. It was a pretty weird setup with lots of dead area on either side of a wide-open vertical space. We knocked down walls and made one side field turf and the other side a weight room. We now had a great location and space but no weights and no equipment.

My partner and I had little to no credit (and a limited credit history as well) but knew we had to see what funding we could get so we could keep our business alive. Thankfully we did not need much because, after all, we started outside with no weights or major equipment. To make it all work, we were able to charge our credit cards and get business lines of credit. It was the first time I had ever seen so much money change hands, thousands and thousands of dollars, that only ever appeared as "meaningless" numbers on a banking or credit card statement. It was all getting more real than I could have ever imagined. I only knew my partner for a year, roughly the same amount of time as when we formed our business. He was a friend, yes, but still a bit of a stranger—someone I was knee deep in business with. We both had a grand idea, to help bring fitness to the masses at an affordable price, but the truth was neither of knew that much about starting or running a business.

Future success seemed difficult but not out of reach either. And if all failed, I could always file bankruptcy as well—which, admittedly, seemed a bit drastic, and I would have had to quit on myself for this to happen. It was all a bit nerve wracking that would, at times, bring up the questions and pain and stories I had heard from my youth—what I had been trying so hard for so long to get away from.

Just before our grand opening, we were able to get a few local newspapers to do a write up about each of us, my partner and I, as well as our business model and our new facility. The story the newspapers told was that of two guys who started with nothing, just an idea and working out on dirt and grass, and who now had a whole building with their name out front. We started to hear chatter around town about those "little boot camp boys" as if we were two train conductors from the children's book and parable, *The Little Engine That Could.* My partner and I "thought we could" and now here we were.

It was now opening day. We had press. We had a new and beautiful facility. And we had mounds and mounds of debt to pay back to the banks.

CHAPTER FOUR

Touch and Go

Just after opening our new facility and for the next few months, more and more clients began to trickle in. It took some time, but slowly our facility, our classes, and our weight room filled up. We had an affordable business model in a community that couldn't pay high prices for fitness (or for much of anything else, for that matter). Besides, me and my partner, never felt right taking too much money when in reality, what we did truly required the other person to do all the work—we were just the voice and the framework.

We tried to build out our community connections to grow our business, because despite all of the foot traffic in our new facility and all the good we were doing bringing fitness to the masses; we just weren't making enough money to survive.

First, we offered clients, whether it was personal training or classes, an incredibly flexible schedule, but that didn't seem to move the needle and help us in any way. It was as if potential customers were scared off as if what we were doing and the price we were offering was "too good to be true." Next, we tried to recruit new personal trainers to work with us and for us. Many who we contacted didn't respond. Some trainers said they did not believe they would make money while others said our prices were too cheap for them to come. It was confusing to me and my partner because some of these people we contacted we knew personally and grew up with. We were all young and go-getters and knew each other—it should have made perfect sense to team up. But these people never even came to our gym or gave us a shot.

For the past few years (even before having our gym), we won so many community awards for best personal training and best weight loss. We were doing great work. Yet many people we knew personally never even showed up to our new facility. We would even see our family and friends posting online looking for a trainer when they knew full well we had a beautiful new gym and well-respected trainers. They simply rejected us.

As two black businessmen, even black people rejected us. Some of the people in the black community would outright tell us that we thought we were, "all that," or too stuck up. But we never thought or even acted like we were better than anyone else. How could we? We were two struggling black entrepreneurs who didn't have the luxury of treating anyone poorly or looking down on others. We were still at the bottom of the business food chain ourselves.

During this time I began to see the world as a cruel place, more so than I had ever really considered. I couldn't rely on for friends and family for morale support or business support. And despite what I had heard from my parents as a child, that black people always should and always do support black businesses—it seemed like a lie and another long-held belief I got from them that just didn't add up. My partner and I would often say that if just five percent of the black community supported us, we would be rich. At this time, when my cynicism toward the world was growing larger, I would tell my partner that we were living on a slave plantation because ninety-eight percent of our clients were white or something other than black. And these people who were our clients, loved, supported, and honored us.

Unfortunately, many leaders within the black community would often try to use us as pawns to host events so they could get more people to buy into whatever it was they were selling. These people would never step inside our gym or support us but wanted to use us because we were young, black men who could be seen as positive influences in what was and is a low income community. They wanted us to minister to youth but they didn't actually support the people they were bringing to talk to us.

Little by little our business started to sustain itself. My partner and I were operating on very slim margins, but we were able to start paying back our creditors, and we were able to take very small salaries for ourselves as well. We weathered many storms because we had a strong core—a solid work ethic, the desire to do good at an affordable price, not to mention many faithful clients, some of whom were signing up for years' worth of services at a time. The "boot camp" boys were coming up bigger than many people ever thought.

At about the halfway through our third year, my partner and I started to notice that certain things about the business weren't going how we wanted. Even though some parts were going well, we both still worked a second job to make ends meet for ourselves. Each of us couldn't always be at the gym, so we weren't running it blind but we weren't able to be as hands on as we would have liked. Oftentimes we would have to come in (taking sick time or paid vacation from our other jobs) and fix things or fire people or give refunds or make adjustments to things about our business that we had no expertise in. We would simply do our best to make the right call depending on the situation.

However, things started to turn when I began to notice that the operation was getting too big not to have either me or my partner on site on a full time basis.

At that time in my life, though, I was twenty-five-years-old with a long term and steady girlfriend and was father to our two young babies. I was traveling for work with my main job and source of income and was making really great money. Factor in a growing side hustle, Frame Fitness, and it all became a bit too much for one person to handle. Of course, I was committed to my girlfriend and babies, but I had to make a decision—stick with my main job, as unfulfilling as it was, or go all in with Frame Fitness, which was more of a wild card financially but something I was fully passionate about. No matter what, a sacrifice had to be made.

As I began to contemplate how to best move forward, I noticed that my work travel had gradually increased and I was away from home, from my girlfriend and two small children, for weeks at a time. I used to enjoy leaving town for work, but my life had changed and I wanted to be around my young family as much as possible. Leaving a mother of two alone for weeks at time while I chased the almighty dollar (making more money than my parents ever made) didn't make sense to me any longer. Being present for them meant more to me than the money I was making.

If I left my job to work at the gym, I would be taking a massive pay cut. This would mean no more extras or luxuries—just living above survival, paying bills, and taking care of the essentials. Luckily, I never cared about material things. Sometimes I just bought things to see what it felt like now that I could afford it. But the truth was that they were just things and a waste of money. Material things did nothing for me inside or out.

After a month or so of serious contemplation about my family, my future, and my work; I was still no closer to coming to a decision. But I knew I needed to figure something out soon. I was juggling way too much and it was wearing me down emotionally and physically. I needed help but I didn't really trust anyone enough to ask for it; I had been hurt and betrayed by people so many times in the past. But I started to recognize that because of the pain and hurt I experienced at the hands of others, I was too quick to blame other people whenever something in life didn't go according to plan or whenever something difficult came up that I didn't know how to deal with. But that mindset was not going to help me move forward in life—for my career, for my girlfriend and babies, and for my emotional wellbeing.

I had to take a stand, to learn to become accountable, and to start trusting in something or someone other than myself. The only thing I ever heard and knew to be true was God and His Word. Neither had failed me yet. So, I decided it was time to make some changes and to do something that was truly positive and life-changing; it was time to become baptized.

CHAPTER FIVE

New Faith

I always heard my elders and grandparents say that giving your life to Christ is the greatest thing you could do, and that it was life changing. I was in need of some direction and guidance, and hopefully my decision to become more spiritual and embrace my Christian roots would help. I just needed to find a good church that would help me along in my new journey.

I started out by going to my business partner's church a few times but I'd didn't like it. The church's sound system was terrible, and anytime I thought I heard the preacher say anything good, I would have to ask the person next to me to repeat what he said. After the first time I attended my partner's church, I moved closer to the front so I could hear, but it turned out that the sermons being delivered were not what I needed. The preacher wasn't telling me anything I never heard before. After a couple of months I got discouraged and stopped going to church because I knew I needed something more powerful. I needed to get the persistent, negative thoughts that had plagued me since my youth out of my head.

Because I wanted to separate my business life and personal life a bit, I had for many years, worked out at a gym in my neighborhood. I would always see this huge black guy working out at my neighborhood gym with his two sons. They were a very nice looking family and it appeared they had a great bond and that their time in the gym was quality bonding time used to build each other up. The big guy would always talk to his boys, smile, and speak to other gym patrons. Every time I saw this big guy, I always thought to myself, "what a cool dude;" I know a likeminded person when I see one. This gentleman and I would make small talk once in a while but for the most part we just did our own thing and did not interact.

I was on Facebook one day and noticed this big, strong looking black guy sent me a friend request and I accepted. This guy was super well dressed in all of his photos and had a big presence online. I clicked on his profile and dig a little deeper and noticed he was a pastor. I was shocked. I didn't know church people worked out, let alone a church person being so committed to fitness that they got as huge as my new pastor friend. The next time I bumped into him I made sure to connect with him. "Why didn't you tell me you were a pastor?" I said, seeking him out from across the gym.

As soon as I reached him, we shook hands firmly. He smiled and said, "you never asked me what I did."

Once again I found myself challenging the assumptions I had learned during my youth about life—that just because you speak to someone they would or should tell you what they do for a living.

"I'm just here working out like you and everyone else," the pastor continued on, his smile never leaving his face. "What does my career have to do with anything? I'm just a pastor and you do whatever it is you do for work outside of this gym. There's no difference."

This guy definitely seemed cooler than your average church person or pastor. The next few times I saw him I let him know I was interested in coming to visit and check out his church. He would simply say, "cool, come on down," but nothing else. He just left it at that; he didn't try to convert me or make me see his world view on spirituality and religion. On one hand it was nice that this guy let me be free to be me and come down to his church whenever I was ready. On the other hand I was also looking for some kind of confirmation that he wanted me to come to his church or at least invite me, but never did.

Week after week I told this pastor I was coming to his church, but I'm not sure he actually believed me after a while. I'm not sure I believed myself either and it started to bother me. I wasn't following through with my word and that felt like a lie and lying to a pastor felt even worse. After the sixth week, I told him I was coming and with a friendly smile he simply said, "You'll come when you're ready." And I did that very Sunday.

My experience at this pastor's church was mind blowing. It was something I had never experienced before. It was as if the pastor was talking directly to me and the whole sermon was about me. The church was thirty-five minutes away and I always told myself I would never drive that for any church yet here I was ready to go back next Sunday.

Later that week at the gym, I told the pastor how amazing his sermon was. He smiled and said, "if you like it so much then come back. There's of that more waiting on you."

Now, every Sunday I would far out of my way to hear this pastor speak, and it felt like he was destroying my insides with his powerful messages. Until I heard this man preach I never before felt that God loved me, and I had never felt that my past could be healed and my present could be fixed and I could actually be the person I was called to be. I was finally sold on church, this particularly church, as well as this pastor.

By this time I had started calling this pastor almost every day and we began hanging out and working out together, too. I was still pretty shocked that a church person, much less a pastor, could be so cool, fly, and young. I decided that this was the guy who I wanted to baptize me. I even called my sister just to double check and make sure we hadn't been baptized as young kids. Finally, I asked my pastor if he would baptize me and he agreed but said he had to look over his church calendar to find a proper date. He also told me, "we have a Daniel fast coming up. I think it would be good for you to try."

I looked at him, my eyes glazed over, because I had no idea what he was talking about. I had no idea who or what Daniel was, and I never did a fast unless it was related to fitness. He could tell I was confused and broke it down for me in homeboy terms. "This is how you get close to God," he began to explain. "Cleanse your body and watch your mind become free. In return you will hear Him speak to you. No meat, wine, or rich foods for twenty-one days. You've got this."

Admittedly I wasn't very excited to eliminate meat and some of my favorite rich foods but I knew I needed to get my mind right and hearing from God in some way had to be a good thing. I actually looked online to see what I could eat and it was very little. Initially I felt like I was about to become a bird for the next three weeks and drink lots of water. But after some more research and consideration I decided that this could be a great time to try a vegan diet, show my clients its benefits, and perhaps even get something positive and spiritual out of the experience.

While in the middle of my fast, the pastor finally told me he would be baptizing me the day the fast ended. I told him, "you might have to dunk me under the water twice because I'm jacked up for real."

He laughed and said he would make sure the first and only time dunking me under the water would count. After the baptism, I received a certificate of completion and decided I would honor my grandparents with this gift. It had always meant so much to them that me and my siblings stayed in church.

A few weeks after my baptism, I thought my life would have changed dramatically. But nothing had really changed. I felt the same—stuck, caught in a dilemma between staying at my job where I traveled too much or quitting and taking a salary cut and working at the gym I co-owned, and the pain and hurt from my childhood still taking over my mind all too often.

I needed answers and I needed the kind of change in my life that would actually stick.

CHAPTER SIX

Seeds of a New Restaurant

After a few more weeks of ruminating on whether I should stay in my job or leave and work full time at my gym, it hit me that I could reach out to my pastor and ask him what I should do.

When I approached my pastor before working out together one day, he gave me his typical silly smile and asked, "What did God tell you to do?"

"How exactly am I supposed to talk with Him?" I asked. "I'm new at all this and still learning how to be a believer in Christ." I was a new student, a baby, when it came to spiritual things.

"Prayer is how you communicate, my man," my pastor said, his voice becoming a little more serious after seeing that my impending decision was weighing heavily on me. "Cast all your problems or cares on Him, and He will answer them."

"Well, I do pray and ask God what I should do."

"And what is it that God has told you to do?" my pastor asked.

"I think He's telling me to quit my job and work on my fitness business," I said.

"Congratulations," my pastor said with a wide grin and then put his hand up to give me a high five.

I was confused. "What's so great about me walking away from a high paying job I work for six months that pays me for an entire year?"

My question was met with another smile. "What you did, or what you're about to do is step out because of faith. Your decision was and is never about money. It's about faith. Believe in Him and He will believe in you."

I took what my pastor said to heart and dove into my journey as an entrepreneur headfirst. I was both the boss and a hustling and hardworking employee. Things actually started off pretty well. I was making an enough money to survive and I wasn't working as often as I initially thought I would. My perspective on life changed a bit. I was home more. I had more freedom. I could pick my kids up and take them to school. I started to do the things I always dreamed of doing and the money wasn't all that important. Spending time with my family was good for my soul. What I had was enough and "enough" was good enough. The business was back on track. I even started to learn more about who I was in Christ.

I started to understand that life didn't have to be all about working forty or more hours a week. I started to see what other business owners and bosses knew. They were too smart to work for anyone and working long hours for little bit of money was insanity. For years, I worked for other people, often times at places I did not want to be. I would put in for time off and get rejected; only able to get a measly few days off per year. Growing up I always heard that working was life but yet I saw people retire in their sixties only to have to get a part time job during retirement to make ends meet. It seemed outrageous to be grinding your whole life just to end up in a situation like that. I always wondered how I could get on the other side of that equation; working for me instead of someone else.

Quitting my job and working on and at my business was the best thing I could have done for myself and my family. Instead of being a part time dad because I was working full time, I was now working reasonable hours and a full time dad and living life full time as well. I now had the freedom to think about things other than my immediate circumstances; I could think and project toward the future. This led me to pitch an idea to my business partner about opening up a restaurant with him.

I actually told my partner about this when I first met him but he laughed it off and shot it down. I brought it up again because I couldn't stop thinking about it and the idea seemed too good to pass up. Opportunities happen when you can see a gap or the missing piece. I knew exactly the concept of restaurant I wanted us to create, and it would fill a need because it was the same type everyone went to outside of this city—in essence it would bring in both customers from our town who wanted a restaurant like this but could also bring in customers from neighboring cities as well. My business partner finally agreed to research and look into my idea.

It felt like a lot, having our gym and barely surviving and then trying to open a restaurant with no prior knowledge on how to do so; but because of my personal growth due to getting involved in church and scripture, I had faith that we could make it work. I started to talk about my idea to people other than my business partner, perhaps trying to "speak it into existence," but was often met with skepticism and the question, "what do you know about restaurants?" My response was always the same: "I've had a kitchen my whole life and many people have eaten my food and loved it. So, it's the same thing just bigger." The skeptics would then find any other reason to question my restaurant concept like—it's too hard to get a liquor license, ninety percent of businesses fail within one year, or restaurants don't make money. I stopped telling certain people about the restaurant concept because almost everyone made themselves out to be an expert, yet never opened a business in their life much less a restaurant.

Luckily my business partner was sold on my idea. Almost immediately we started looking for investors. Our plan beyond taking on investment money was to do as much leg work as possible, learn on the fly (while spending as little money as possible to acquire knowledge), and then figure out what we don't know or don't have. Initially we knew we didn't have the resources or know-how to bring this restaurant to life, but we both felt if we believed it would happen then it would happen.

When we first built our gym the contractor who did the work always said how he wanted to invest or do something else with his money. So we pitched the idea to him about opening a restaurant and what the returns looked like. We thought we were being smart by doing this. We could hire him as a contractor or make him a partner whose investment in the restaurant would be completing the construction. He would tell us often about how well he was doing and he would mention he had enough money to buy a Bentley, which cost $300 thousand or more. Having this contractor on board was like taking out two birds with one stone. Thankfully he agreed to be a part of our project.

The three of us began meeting weekly at my gym to come up with a plan and pull off the "unthinkable." We started searching high and low for a space for our restaurant that wouldn't cost us too much in rent. It took us months to find what we were looking for; a place we could call home. What we finally found was an empty space. It would have to do.

We pooled our money together for the deposit for the space and the first few months' rent. We began accumulating a little bit of restaurant equipment, truly not much, and our contractor partner began work on construction. Everything was done from the ground up—the kitchen, the bar, and even the bathrooms. The unknown started to become known, which also meant we began to realize that our budget was growing rapidly and getting a little out of control. Expenses started to pile up, and my gym partner and I started to worry because we didn't have a lot of money. Our contractor partner began to self-fund certain elements (more than just construction) during this phase and it was taking its toll on him and our collective partnership. Luckily, my gym partner and I were able to find a few smaller investors to give us some much needed capital during this time. For a period of a month or so after this, our contractor partner seemed much less on edge and easy to work with.

But soon enough our new investment money was eaten up and our contractor partner began to get testy about everything, even putting up his other business as a guarantor to acquire some of the equipment we needed. Delays on construction began to grow longer and longer and the three of us started to resort to bickering and finger pointing. Our project built on faith, love, and trust was now being sullied by fear, pride, and ego. If something didn't change soon, our restaurant concept would implode before it event started, losing tens of thousands of dollars for our investors as well as our partnership and friendships, and even putting our main livelihoods at risk.

CHAPTER SEVEN

Three is a Crowd

I decided that me and my two partners needed to sit down together in the same place to meet and discuss and figure out how we could move forward more easily without arguing or playing the blame game. We started as a "three headed monster" taking on whatever roles we had to take on, and we never really worried about the cost. I knew our construction partner had (or at he said he had) a lot of money and wealth and so I assumed that cost wasn't an issue for him, which in hindsight was a mistake. He started to feel left out to dry because costs were mounting quickly but didn't speak up about it until he exploded at us. As of late my gym partner had been serving as the middleman and lightning rod between me and our other partner, and all the back and forth was starting to take its toll on my well-being.

After the three of us got together, it became clear to me that my gym partner had a pretty similar mindset as I did—

let's work together and let's make this restaurant happen no matter what because we were all already neck deep in it. But it also became clear that while our construction partner was a good guy, he was starting to lose faith in the project and in me and our other partner, which was causing his ego to inflate and causing him (and all of us) a great deal of tension and stress. His fears about the restaurant were infecting his mind, in a way, and in turn in led him to feeling trapped and angry.

Our construction partner started to demand more money from us, but neither of us had any more money to give, nor did we have any additional collateral to put up to receive any more lines of credit. When we told him this, he insisted on owning a full 40% of the company and that the three of us were no longer equal partners. We argued back and forth but ultimately he had the upper hand—more money than the two of us and control over the aspects of finishing the construction. So, we agreed that he would take 40% and my other partner and me would split the remaining stake in the company equally. But our trust in each other was truly fading away.

It had been such a gift to have had the experience of two strangers meeting and starting a gym together and having it go so well, but then to start off in a similar manner with these two partners only to see things begin to fall apart was very difficult. It also reinforced the story I had always heard that black people could not get along in business. Why couldn't minorities work together? It didn't make sense and I certainly didn't want this "story" to be true.

I also learned during this time that as an entrepreneur, the clock doesn't necessarily stop just because you go home. Work and building your business can be, and sometimes is, a twenty-four hour venture. It became difficult for me to separate work from home; my stress levels clearly negatively affecting the people I loved the most. My time was split between running two business and my home. I was beginning to feel as if I was stretched too thin. I exhausted all my resources and any free time I had, becoming overwhelmed with mental anguish and anxiety over all the things that I felt weren't going well in my life and my businesses. Only a few months prior, I had told my pastor and a few others that I was "living the dream," but now I was "living a nightmare."

Around this time I took on a new personal training client at my gym. I knew of him because I had seen him come in and work out on his own a few times. He was a smart guy and owned a successful business in the area. Whenever he walked in he just looked like money and talked and walked like money. He was clearly very confident and always dressed super sharp. I instantly judged him as being arrogant and conceited. The story I had been told my whole life was that these kinds of people, rich older white men, thought they were above everyone else. I grouped him into every other older rich white person because that's what I had been taught.

Whenever he worked out with me, he would tell me exactly what he wanted to do and how he wanted me to help.

He was pretty self-efficient. We would make a little small talk but I would always try to get him in and out.

One day in the middle of a session a water rep came by to finish the sale of a water cooler I had requested. After signing the paperwork, I became upset and angry at the rep. I felt what we discussed on the phone wasn't what I just signed. When I came back to my rich older white client, my face was clearly colored with anger and frustration and tension.

"Are you okay?" my client asked.

I shrugged him off and told him I was fine. Of course, I was lying to myself and to him.

"You don't look fine," my client replied with a laugh. "It looks like you're pissed the hell off."

I was pretty shocked at his response because he never really spoke like that. I agreed with him and admitted that the water rep pissed me off because I felt like he was trying to take advantage of me. I opened up a little more and explained to my client that it felt like the rep was purposefully misleading me, forcing me to sign some paperwork.

He told me he empathized with me and we then went back to working out. In a matter of moments, though, my client brought it up again. "That guy really set you off," he remarked, to which I agreed.

I couldn't help but wonder why my client wouldn't drop the subject. "You told me what happened," he said, "but I don't understand why you are upset and angry about it. You look fine on the outside but I can tell something big is bubbling underneath."

I just looked at him, puzzled, because I wasn't sure what he was getting at.

With a smile he asked, "Did you read the paperwork before you signed it?"

"Yes, of course."

"Did you read it in full or did you just skim it?"

"I…I skimmed it," I replied.

"A little piece of advice, if I may," he said. I gave a nod of approval for him to continue. "Whenever you have paperwork to sign, read through it in depth. Ask questions about what you don't understand. And you can also take a red pen and cross through the parts of the paperwork that you don't agree with."

What he was saying made perfect sense and I agreed with him.

"That guy's job was to get you to sign the paperwork. You had a choice to sign it or not. He got what he wanted and you got what you signed for."

And in that moment it hit me—I was mad at this rep when I was at fault for not reading. I made that choice and now I was wasting energy and getting angry with someone for my own actions.

My client then asked me another question. "Have you ever had times in your life where you felt the way you were feeling today, like with that rep, and had similar thoughts of anger and frustration?"

"Story of my life," I said.

He then came closer and started to speak softly, his every word colored with comfort and care in them. "Did you ever ask yourself why you think the way you do or feel that feeling when you get upset?"

I laughed and said, "yes, all the time. I've had a rough life, at least mentally, and I've always wanted to know why I am the way I am. Maybe that feeling of anger is who I am. I don't necessarily want to be that way but maybe I have no choice."

The next thing he said changed my life forever. "What is everything you know up until this point was a lie? Or maybe parts of it are lies. Would you be willing to explore that possibility?"

"Yes," I said. "Absolutely. I've always wanted to know why I think the way I think."

"Then let's get to work," he said, and then waved me over to a table and pulled out a sheet of paper and a pen. "Time to change your life."

Little did I know that the next hour I spent with him would challenge my belief system, get to the subconscious root of many of the issues that were causing me mental pain, and change the course of my life forever.

CHAPTER EIGHT

Picking Apart the Past

I had always wanted to know why I am the way I am and why I thought the way I thought. No one had ever challenged me or worked with me to have that kind of understanding. I wouldn't have even known where to start or who to reach out to for help with something like this. Whether it was God or plain luck, I felt fortunate to have crossed paths with this training client at my gym, who had volunteered to help me challenge and understand my subconscious thoughts and beliefs. If I could understand this a little better, I had a feeling that life would look a whole lot different, and for the better.

He slid me a sheet of paper and passed me a pen as we sat down at an empty table with him.

"Tell me any other time you felt angry or upset in your life," my client said. "No matter how big or small, just tell me."

I began to open up about everything I could think of that made me angry at one point or another in life. He began writing everything I was saying. Certain memories, for me, stuck out more than others. I told him a story about my childhood where my mother never came to any of my sporting events. I always remembered suiting up to play and the game would about to start and I would be looking all over for my mom, wondering if she was going to show. My dad would always come to my games and when I asked about my mom, he would get a little angry or sarcastic and make it a point to say that work was more important to her than making time for her kids.

My client wrote all of that down and then asked, “Is all of that true?”

“Yes, it’s all true,” I said. “It happened all the time.”

“And your mom worked all the time and your dad spoke in anger or sarcasm about your mom missing your games?”

“Absolutely.”

“Did your mom ever tell you she was coming to your games and didn’t show?

“She would always say she was working but would try to come if she could.”

“Okay,” he said. He then traced his pen to the bottom of the page. He wrote the word “truths” right next to “Sean.”

1. Sean’s mom works all the time.
2. Sean’s dad uses anger in sarcasm when they talk about her not coming to support his games.
3. She told you she would come if she could.

We discussed this for a few more moments and then he asked me what I noticed about the story I was telling him. I read over the paper and replied, "I'm not sure that's exactly how I recall it happening."

All he said was "hmm," and then processed what I was saying. Everything he was saying and doing felt encouraging; he never outright objected or contradicted me. It felt like he was doing his best to truly hear me out. "Look again," he said, "at what you recall to be the story because I disagree with you."

I looked up, smiled, and said, "How would you know? You weren't there."

He laughed aloud and pointed at my chest and said, "YOU were there and don't know."

Once again I was stuck. Not in a mean way, but it felt like he was twisting my words around using them against me.

He looked at me directly in my eyes with a stern face and asked, "Sean, are you ready for this?"

"Yes," I replied. "I am not afraid. I've been looking for what's real my whole life. Give it to me straight."

"Okay Sean," he said. "I'm going to let you have it, but remember, I'm doing nothing wrong and you've done nothing wrong."

This entire conversation he had been speaking that way, always alluding to something but never showing a "full hand," as it were.

"Just tell me," I said. "I can handle it."

"Sean, this is just like the water incident. It's identical. Can you see it?"

I started thinking about both stories; not reading a contract from a water rep and the other about how my mom never showed up to my games. I thought about both, but something about the two just wasn't aligning for me. I had to admit to my client that by comparison, these two incidents could not be identical.

He smiled again. "What if I told you the truth has always been right in front of you and you just couldn't see it? Maybe your story is so messy you cannot even see it yet. However, it has always been right in front of your face."

"I'm really not getting what you're talking about," I said. At this point, I was getting pretty annoyed and just wanted him to give me a straightforward answer. But then time was up and our session was over; my client had to get going.

"Hold onto that paper," he said. "Keep thinking about what we've been talking about and we'll finish next time."

He got up from his seat and I just sat there staring at the table in confusion. Was this guy trying to play a weird mind game with me by having my thoughts racing all day? Thankfully I knew I would see him in two days because we worked out three times per week.

At the start of our next session, my client told me, "let's not workout today. Let's just talk."

"Listen," I said. "I value your time but you are paying me to work out and we got carried away last session talking."

He smiled again. I started to notice he would do that every time he had something smart to say. "It's my money and if I'm paying you, then I get to tell you how I want to spend my session. And I want to use my money and pay to talk to you. Can we continue what we were talking about from last session?"

I started to think this guy is good, very wise and very slick; no wonder he was so successful. I agreed to continue and we dove back into the paper that I had neatly folded into my wallet.

"Did you ever figure out why I disagreed with the story you told me about?" he asked.

I hadn't and then so we went over the story about my mom and dad again.

"Would your mom agree with the story you told?" he asked.

"She wouldn't," I replied.

"And why not?"

"Because she was working and I guess if she could have made it then she would have."

"But Sean, you told me the exact same thing before but you were angry about it. Was she being honest with you?"

A weight on my mind had instantly been lifted. My mom had been telling the truth. Somewhere along the way I hadn't able to see that. Realizing that in that moment made me a little sad and it must have shown on my face.

"Are you okay, Sean?" he asked with true concern. "You just figured something out didn't you?"

"Yes. I did. I'm fine, though."

"Hey man, it's all good. You don't have to tell me anything. We can stop if you want."

"No," I said. All of this felt a bit difficult but it was no time stop. Not now. "We're good. I'm not upset at all."

"Great. Great," he said. "So tell me what you're thinking."

I explained that I realized my mom was telling the truth. And what my dad had been telling me about my mom was only partly true.

"Tell me more," he said.

I went on and stated that the part about my dad telling me mom didn't care was the part that wasn't true. That was his reality. Not my mom's and not my own. My mom gave me her story and she was honest and consistent with it. And then my head started spinning fast.

For the first time in my life, I had clarity. I had held this grudge against my mom my whole life based on words someone else fed me. She had done nothing wrong. And even though what my dad had told me wasn't helpful and a bit detrimental, what he did wasn't wrong either. Everyone was only doing what he or she thought was right for his or her life. That's it. I started replaying events beginning from my childhood and it was a lot to take in.

What other people and situations had I judged or taken offense to because I misread what was happening or because I wasn't able to empathize and realize whatever they were doing wasn't a direct attack on me? It had me thinking about my parents, my babies, my friendships, and every aspect of my two businesses.

It was the first time in my life I had a true and utter breakthrough. And I was ready to uncover a whole lot more.

CHAPTER NINE

Releasing the Past

I would see my training client three times a week as usual, but it got to the point that we stopped working out together. He kept paying me but all he wanted to do was talk and help me out. To him, money didn't matter—helping me was his mission. It felt like one of those few times in life, that I was aware of, when you knew you were on the right track with something because someone would come out of nowhere and start helping you stay on the right track. I noticed that these kinds of things only happened when I was on a mission and walking by faith and not by sight. And this was one of those times.

Over a few weeks we continued to talk about my past, specifically my family, to continue to help me grow during this period where I was having such a big personal breakthrough.

One day, we began discussing some of the stories I held based on other authority figures, whether it was in school, or work, or society.

My mind instantly went to the time I survived a cop putting a gun to my head. It was a time when I was traveling in my car on a small local highway to get to my gym. It was early morning, around 4 a.m. and I needed to go in and get paperwork done before opening the gym to the public at 5 a.m. While on my way, a police car flew by me with lights on and then slowed down, cut off its lights, and then turned and followed behind me.

I took an exit ramp not more than one hundred feet away and the cop car trailed slowly behind me. I figured this car was going to stop me eventually, so I did what I heard to do on news outlets, being that I was a black male and it was early morning and dark outside. I knew that just off this exit was a gas station so I decided to head there. With all the police shootings of black men in America, I was taught to always pull over, if instructed to do so, into a safe and well-lit area. The gas station would serve that purpose.

The exit had an immediate red light and the cop was the next car behind me. I stopped and when it finally turned green, I slowed all the way down maybe going 15 mph. I then turned on my hazard lights letting him know I was aware and that I saw him. Finally I pulled into the gas station. The cop followed directly behind me and then he turned his lights back on signaling I was being pulled over or about to be questioned. As soon as I pulled my key from the ignition, I made sure to text my business partner to let him know where I was and what was happening—you can never be too careful.

Almost immediately I looked in my rear view mirror and I heard footsteps racing toward me. By time I looked out my window, which I made sure was already down, the cop had already approached with his gun out, for no reason, and had it pointed inside my car, directly at my head. He began to shout, "hands up where I can see them," and kept saying it.

I tossed up my hands and asked, "Why do you have a gun at my head?"

He stated that I didn't pull over when he cut his lights back on the interstate. Of course, that didn't make sense. You don't turn your lights off to pull someone over, and from where I was on the interstate to the gas station wasn't more than thirty seconds. But he was super irritated and kept his gun out and began to ask for my driver's license over and over.

At the same time, I was pretty upset because I knew I had done nothing wrong, and I'm pretty sure that an annoyed and angry look was showing on my face and the cop didn't like it. "How am I supposed to grab my license if you keep asking me to show you my hands?" I asked.

He didn't want to hear it and kept asking for my license and registration. I had to suck up my pride and be super careful. I began to rummage through some paperwork on my front seat to find my wallet so I could give him my license. I also had to dig through paperwork in my glove compartment so I could find the registration. It felt like it took me forever to find both of those items, all the while he still had a gun pointed at my head.

He took my ID and went back to his car and I made sure to continue texting my business partner, who also happened to be a cop, asking him to come help and deescalate the situation. My gym was right behind the gas station and my partner should have been close by.

The cop returned in about five minutes and handed me a ticket telling me I was speeding down the interstate when I knew I wasn't. "So you're going to ask me to sign this ticket and just act like you didn't put a gun to my head?" I asked.

"Exactly," he said nonchalantly. "Sign it."

"I'm not signing anything until someone with some authority can explain how you can just pull a gun on someone for no reason. Just because they feel like it."

"If you don't sign it, then I will take you in and you'll be put in jail."

"I have the right to ask for your supervisor to come here and discuss this with him or her," I stated.

The cop backed off and went to his car. A few moments later another cop car showed backing him up but then my partner arrived and approached. The first cop I had dealt with told my friend to back off and then asked who he was, what he wanted, and what he was doing there.

My partner explained he was "on the job" and I was his friend, that he had heard I was about to get shot, and that this was all just a misunderstanding.

After a few moments, my partner approached with my ticket and asked me to sign and then told me we would talk about it later. But I was heated. I did everything right and "by the book" and still I got a gun to my head and a ticket for no reason.

As I signed the ticket the first officer I had dealt with leaned into my car and whispered, "I'm sorry this happened. I've been working 60-80 hours per week the last few weeks without a day off. I'm just tired."

I couldn't believe his words—the one who should be protecting and serving can't be tired and pulling a gun out. He asked me to try and understand and have compassion for him and that he was sorry.

Ultimately, he told me to go to court and he would have my ticket thrown out, but he didn't follow through on his promise. The judge agreed that the officer pulling his gun on me had nothing to do with my "speeding." Once again, White America won.

I shared this story with my rich white client, and he was shocked and appalled at what happened. He expressed compassion. And just like we had with other stories from my past he asked me to break down what was truth and what was the story I had created in my mind.

The story in my mind was that white cops in America don't care about blacks and can do anything and get away with it. I then stated the truth is that nothing is all that wrong. I was alive and able to tell my story. At one point I was hurt and upset but that was just my pride and ego. The cop had only done what he felt was best at that time based on the information he had in his mind. I was just a character in the story he was playing out. It was unfortunate but I didn't get shot. I was hurt because I was choosing to dwell on the story that happened and added a bunch of "what ifs" and using my imagination to create a new story that never actually happened. I laughed a little because the conclusion we came to actually made sense. Every question I had ever had about my life had logical answers.

I started to see how much pride and ego could influence the stories we tell ourselves. That's why we suffer; because the mind plays tricks on us. To close our session he asked me to tell him something that made happy. I told him just seeing my kids made me happy. He then patted me on the back and told me he was looking forward to seeing my in two days.

The inner work I was doing with my client was only the tip of the iceberg. More epiphanies had to be coming soon, and it was exciting to see where they would lead and how they would change life for the better.

CHAPTER TEN

New Stories

The stories I had held onto for so many years, the ones I told myself were fact and that had caused me a lot of pain; they were now just stories and I was able to consider that there were so many other angles to what I had experienced. It caused an almost immediate release of the suffering inside my head; it had disappeared.

I shared this exact same thought with my client and he asked me how I felt about it.

"Great, actually," I said. "As weird as it might sound. I waited many years for this. It's time I can never get back, which is a little sad."

"You're twenty-eight, Sean," he said. "Look how quickly you discovered your truth. I'm fifty years old have only recently started to feel better about the stories I've carried with me my entire life."

"I guess it could have been worse," I said with a laugh. "I could be you."

My client smiled and knew I was only teasing. "The beautiful thing you have now is awareness. The stories in your past, they're just stories. They're all in your mind. Touch the ground. Your body can feel that. That's reality. The rest is perception that comes from your mind."

It was in that moment that I started to understand his first question, "what if everything you knew up until this point was a lie?" It was almost the exact sentiment as what my pastor had first conveyed to me when we first met. I was gaining truth and wisdom from both God and man. It was a little spooky but also very liberating. In a way it reminded me of the old phrase, "The teacher appears when the student is ready."

The sum total of where I was in life was due to my thought life and my actions that followed. I started to feel responsible for all the things I had blamed others for, which allowed me to move forward in life with more effective and efficient actions, and with much better relationships with both myself and others.

Working with my client, he even challenged me on the lighter side of things too. We talked about my kids and I told him it makes me happy just seeing them; their smiles and their sense of freedom to be carefree. We broke down what all that meant and if the story I was telling was one hundred percent true. After unwrapping it all, I was able to come to the conclusion that my kids did not make me happy; I was choosing to be happy and decided to think happy thoughts about them.

I had wondered aloud to my client why I had never been taught any of this. It now felt like I couldn't be completely certain about anything.

"Why is that?" he asked.

"Well, for one, I can't actually control the outcome. I can only then control my actions. I can't even control my mind," I said with a laugh.

"Not true," he said with a smile. "Yes, you can't control the outcome. That means you have to walk by faith. But you can control your mind, and how you react to what life throws your way. You get to choose to learn a lesson from any situation or make meaning from it. Like your happiness over your children, you get to choose that, which you, in fact, have done."

I realized he was completely right. I alone had control over my mind and over thought processes I never knew existed. If I wanted to be happy, I had to cultivate that feeling in my mind; not just wait for the feeling to come over me as a result of something out of my control.

I started to see that I was never taught about the school of life and I had been flunking a course that, up until that point, I wasn't even aware I was taking. I now understood that without training the mind, the stories we tell ourselves sometimes can cloud our thinking. My spirit began to shift, learning how to process my thoughts and what I was actually in control of. Our belief system is what runs our life and when we believe in anything enough we will take action to make it happen. I was now fighting a battle that I had the tools to win.

At times, my girlfriend would always ask me why I was the way I was. I hardly ever showed her compassion. I never cuddled with her. I didn't like her or anyone touching my hands. I would prefer that she had her space and I had mine. She would always try to be understanding, but I never could express the right words to help her do so. All I ever said to her, and often, was, "this is who I am." I had no idea until my mental breakthrough with my client, that I did not know how to do any of those things—to be compassionate, intimate, vulnerable, and expressive.

These were all examples of "healthy learned behaviors" that I had never seen consistently, nor did I have a positive role model growing up to help me learn. My girlfriend had wanted something from me that I didn't know how to give. I wanted her to accept me as I was and am and was hurting because I felt like she wouldn't. My mind was so cloudy, I didn't realize I could have given her more. I dragged an innocent person into my mental warzone. I was hurting from my past and needed to heal and to learn. But the good news was that I wasn't bad or stupid or messed up; I was just temporarily uneducated about these things.

I started to look inward and at every angle of every one of my relationships with anyone in my present and past. It scared me a bit because all the hurts I had felt were only my perceptions, and the stories I had told myself. And I now knew that not only did I have some healing to do, but I had to set healing in motion for relationships I had with people I loved.

As I was learning and processing and uncovering the truth about past stories from my life, I still had one business to run, my gym, and another to build, my restaurant.

Unfortunately, the gym was becoming unsustainable and more and more difficult to run. The business wasn't making enough money to be profitable and to afford our employees in addition to my salary. At the same time, I really wanted the restaurant to succeed. I knew it would cost another several thousand dollars to continue to build it from the ground up and get it open and running. It was a daunting task to think about where the money would come from. But I believed and had faith that we could somehow make this happen. This would be a new chapter and new story in my life. As long as I stuck to the truth and told and interpreted the right story about the restaurant, then all would be well. It was time to start writing the story that I wanted to tell.

CHAPTER ELEVEN

Miracles

Over the next several weeks, I began unpacking my entire life and worked through every past memory that caused me pain, fear, hurt, and heartache. My perspective began to change. I no longer judged people or situations and I stopped playing the victim. I no longer assumed I knew all the details and doing so made it easier to understand other people. I could hear their words and in return, I could sense the pain that was influencing them when they spoke.

During this time, my pastor informed me he was looking to start a church in my city. He would often ask me to help him find property. I suggested that that should use my gym. I had an open field made of turf. All the church needed was chairs. Church is not a location anyway; it's what's in your heart and mind.

I suggested multiple times that he use my gym, but ultimately he told me he was fine and he and the church elders had something else in mind. But several weeks after turning me down, my pastor came back to me and asked if my offer was still available. Of course, I said "yes."

If I could do anything major in life, other than being a father and friend and business owner, it would be helping to start a church. To me there was nothing better than being a part of transforming my community for good and helping to nourish the spiritual side of life for people.

My pastor asked me what it would cost for his new church to rent my gym.

"It's free," I replied, to which he looked shocked and amazed. "You changed my life. And there's no way I can charge you or ever hope to repay you. I just want to help you do what you do, so you can change other people's lives, too."

He pleaded with me to allow him to pay a small fee or some kind of rent because he knew my situation with the gym and that it was on the verge of closing down. But I refused to take his money; it just seemed like the right thing to do at the time. Sometimes he would bless me with a check but I never wanted to make it about me. I always felt like money took the heart out most things and I had to pay same bills anyway. My parents started charging me rent soon as I turned eighteen, which was confusing because I never understood how my money was needed to pay the same bills just because I turned eighteen. They would say that paying rent was teaching me to be responsible, and that I couldn't move anywhere for free. Unlike my parents, I didn't feel like I needed to teach the church fiscal responsibility, and so they would be my very own rent free tenant.

Over the next few weeks and months, I felt like I had a renewed spirit and much clearer mind. My gym was still running, even though just barely. The church was up and running. And my restaurant was really coming along even though I still had some conflict with my construction partner. Everything was starting to come into place. I felt like I had everything I wanted and yet I still had nothing. I had much less money in the bank than ever before.

One unexpected benefit of my newfound personal growth; I started to attract good and positive energy from the people around me. I began to witness real life blessings and things that some might call "supernatural."

One day while at my gym, I had new female client come in. She mentioned she found the gym by way of the church my pastor started there. I asked her if she was local, and she said she just moved to town. She told me she searched for the gym for two months prior to her coming to church. "Why didn't you use GPS?" I asked.

"I tried," she said with a laugh. "But somehow I could never find it."

I thought that was strange as she continued telling me her story.

"You won't believe this," she said. "I was telling my mother a dream about a dream I had and I feel like I need to tell you. I had a dream that I was at a church with a green floor."

My eyes got big because my gym, this church, had green field turf as a floor. She then mention the chairs being a dark color, maybe burgundy. I started backing up. I had green flooring and burgundy chairs. After the dream, she somehow stumbled upon the church. She said it wasn't until after her first service that she looked for the name on the building and noticed it was a gym—the same gym she was looking for the past two months with GPS.

"Crazy," was all I could say. I couldn't believe what I was hearing. "You couldn't find the gym using GPS but had a dream about a church, only to find out my facility was both a church and a gym."

"Yes," she said with a smile. "There's a different energy in here; you guys have an anointing on your life."

"Thank you," I said. "I believe we do."

People started to see on the outside what I felt on inside. It was a great feeling.

We still needed more money to finish the restaurant, and walking by faith, I was able to get a few clients to invest double digit amounts into me for the restaurant to finish. Both clients said they never cared much about the restaurant but believed in me and my gym partner. They saw each of us working so hard and they knew we would not quit based on what they saw.

When one door opens, another door closes, and in this case it was our gym. Business continued to slow down. Our lease was up at the end of the year and we knew we likely could not afford to continue. It got to the point where we had to stop paying our rent. We also got very far behind on bills. As usual, we still kept the business going believing all things would work out, even though we knew in our heart of hearts the business wouldn't survive. My new mindset was helping me work through my gym business failing—I couldn't control everything but I could control my mindset, some of the outcome, and how I reacted to it all.

My business partner and I came up with an idea that before we closed we would sell all of our equipment to pay back all the money we owed. And we owed quite a bit, especially to our landlord, who would call us every week asking where our money was. We would simply reply that when we got some money we would hand it over. We eventually stopped responding and they stopped asking. It was almost end of the lease and we would have to deal with paying him the money at some point. During the second to last month, our landlord sent us a letter in the mail notifying he was suing us for thirty thousand dollars in unpaid fees. We didn't have it, and in the past I would have let that stress me out and cause me to act out toward others. But something, perhaps my new mindset, allowed me to feel somehow it would all get taken care of.

About five weeks before the end of our lease, a woman came in and inquired about the equipment we were selling. She asked the price and we told her thirty thousand for everything, which was an incredible deal. She agreed with a handshake, putting my and my partner's minds at ease. We were going to walk away from this gym free and with a clean slate. It made the process of shutting down much easier.

However, two weeks later, as we started preparing to get some of the equipment wrapped up and shipped out, this lady who was buying our equipment called and told us she couldn't afford to buy all of our equipment but could still take some of it. We had already burnt weeks not advertising to sell our equipment and now we were hard pressed to sell. This lady only took several thousand dollars of equipment. We were still under a thirty thousand dollar lawsuit with no way to pay it or for lawyer's fees, otherwise we were completely liable for every dollar. We needed a miracle…and fast.

CHAPTER TWELVE

Keeping My Mind Right

My partner and I had to scramble and began to make online ads to try and sell the equipment so we could pay off our debt. I don't know how we did it but in two days, we sold about seventeen thousand dollars' worth of equipment. Neither of us thought initially that we could sell our equipment that fast but we believed and it happened. We even sold another several thousand dollars' worth of equipment to a client by putting them on a payment plan. Things were looking up but we still had a long way to go to pay off our debt.

We were also hanging by a thread with the restaurant but we got another few investors and that went a long way toward us finally opening the restaurant.

We were stretched pretty thin, but still had the seventeen thousand dollars from selling our equipment. I told my partner that I didn't want to give all of it to our landlord; that we should hold onto it and see what we can settle for. We were going to play broke and see what happened and my partner agreed. The two of us concluded that we would offer our landlord three thousand to settle our thirty thousand dollar bill. We first told our real estate agent what we wanted to do. He agreed but pointed out that they could take our offer as an insult; then he put forward our offer several days later.

Luckily, I was still able to bring in a little income by training a few of my gym clients at the high school we used when we first started out. My gym partner happened to be on the premises while I was working out with my client. Not long into my session, my partner ran in jumping up and down and told me to come outside.

"What is going on?" I asked, peeking my head out of the door, then following him into the hallway.

"Check this out," he said, pointing to his phone. He pulled up an email that he had just gotten only five minutes prior. It was a miracle. Our former landlord who had sued us for thirty thousand dollars had accepted our offer to repay only three thousand dollars. I almost couldn't believe it. Once again, God made a way out of nothing. This was the manifestation of my choice to walk by faith.

Amazingly enough we still had a great deal of training clients, as well as people from our old gym who wanted us to take them back on as clients. There were too many requests and we didn't want to overload the high school we were using. A client of ours owned a huge construction company. He had a compound and we would often train him and his family at their own personal gym. My partner bumped into him one day and he mentioned that we could use his facility whenever we needed. Again, another blessing landed on our doorstep. He told us we didn't have to pay a dime, to just sign a waiver and continue to be great. He was a God-fearing man like me and my partner and always admired our push to get what we wanted and liked our mission—health and to help the community.

At this time, I finally made a decision about my restaurant. I decided I would leave it behind, sell my shares, and walk away. The thing I dreamed about doing for ten years finally came to life. It only took one year of planning and eight months of building. I finally understood this restaurant was not about me—I had no money to pay for anything. I believed in my vision and got others to believe and provide resources. But one partner didn't believe we were all together; it takes a village to build or grow anything and this guy wanted to be the captain. He spent two hundred thousand dollars on the restaurant and didn't hesitate to remind us all every time we met up or discussed anything. I couldn't work or live like that. I gave them and the restaurant my vision but after that, I wasn't needed and I was at peace with that. Walking away wasn't a failure, my time was simply up and my ego no longer needed me to be involved.

I now had no business and my finances were practically in shambles, but I couldn't have been more at peace with myself. My heart was finally healed and all the wounds from my past were gone. Money never mattered anyway, and I had none, so I was okay. Life was good; I was happy and free. Anyone can have what I had and still have as long as they believe in themselves and put God first; the rest will fall into place.

We as people are here for a good time, not a long time. No matter your circumstances, it's imperative that I and all of us not waste time on fear or taking someone else's word for it. We must explore for ourselves, take risks, and walk through that door to see what's on the other side. Take back the control you unknowingly gave to world. It's your life; make it count. What I have and what you have inside you is worth more than anything on the outside. Renew your mind, heart, and soul. I find I need to do so daily and weekly. The world needs all of us pure in truth and less in hate. We often love strangers more then we love ourselves, and to our own detriment. We keep up with people and things that have nothing to do with us getting where we want to be. These distractions cause us to watch when we should be playing the game. The mind will stay on what you put it on.

Life is full of mysteries and obstacles. Where you started is where you started. Where you came from is where you came from. Your family is your family. There is not much you can do about that, if anything at all. The journey you take from there is simply about you becoming the best version of you as possible. You cannot rewrite the past but what's beautiful is that your future lies inside of you. Those goals or things you daydream about. The places you want to go. The person you ultimately want to be. These are all simple decisions and options that we all have. And it all starts in our mind when our heart becomes attached to the outcome.

Everything you have ever wanted has a simple price. The price in monetary currency is always zero. The price is your effort and your willingness not to quit. Your ability to stay focused while the deafening noise from rest of the world grows louder and louder. It sometimes may seem as if you are behind or not doing enough—but do not grow weary and give up; please carry on.

Your journey is your story and everyone else is a part of your story. You are the main character, the director, the author. The power you've been looking for already lies within you. You have been taught that there are many things you have no control over. You've been told many things that weren't true. You've been shown things you always wanted but have been told at times that these things will forever be out of your reach. But, in reality, that is not true. It is only a matter of when you finally decide that you want something badly enough; then it will come to you. What you believe in your heart will come out; positive or negative, healthy or unhealthy. Believe in peace and you will have peace. Believe in forgiveness and you will have forgiveness. Believe in strength and you will have power. Believe in yourself and you can do all this in Christ who strengths you. Doubt means fear. Faith means unknown. Only you know what you can do when you go after what it is that you want.

These are the principles that help me govern the way I live my life, and you can use them for yourself as well. Whatever I had hoped for as a little boy and young man, it was likely that I was hoping for some kind of fairytale or happy ending. But now I realize I don't need any of that—I am already living my own fairytale and so far it is shaping up to be a great one.

CHAPTER THIRTEEN

Fertilizing a Seed

Have you ever wondered how you got where you are today? Some would say it's because of hard work. Others might say their schooling prepared them for this. A few might even respond with, "I don't know."

Everyone is technically right in their own definition of how they got to where they are. But no matter how you got to where you are, you did so with "seeds." Your thoughts powered by your beliefs has you exactly where you envisioned yourself. Everything happens twice—first in the mind and then in the natural, tangible world. Once we can envision something, we can feel empowered to obtain it in the natural world.

Over the years I've noticed something about myself and my clients; everything seen in the mind hasn't always been obtainable. The thought was there, the excitement was palpable, but for some reason, the effort came up short. The feeling of, "I did everything right and still no grand prize," was often present. One might even engage in internal dialogue such as, "what am I doing wrong? I've done everything they said it took to have the thing I'm working toward. I've checked X off the list." For a long time, I too couldn't comprehend why I would fall short but I eventually discovered that I didn't receive the prize because I quit. I simply stopped working the process because the return didn't come fast enough. I made the mistake and believed that my outcome would be how someone else said it would.

Once I had this revelation, it made me review my life and all the people that gave me instructions who told me about "the prize" yet didn't help prepare me for when the outcome was different. *Go to college, get a degree, and if you do that, you will have the job of your dreams*. Now, I'm wondering why I still believe other people's words to make major decisions with my life. I'm the only one who can see my vision, yet I let everyone around push their own on me. I had a thought, and they had a thought. They somehow assumed their thought for my life was better than mine. I was a walking robot, and I didn't even know it.

From the time we are born the people who raise us speak into our subconscious and conscious. The words they speak are seeds that become planted all through lives in the garden of our mind. We water the ones we think will grow the best and leave the ones we think aren't important to rot. At times, random weeds will grow, destroying a potential harvest. For many of us, we trusted and believed that the people around us were providing the most adequate information for the prosperity of our garden. In truth, the people guiding us only knew what they believed to be true—not necessarily that actual truth. So, release any hate or ill will toward anyone for misguiding us; it's very likely they didn't know any better. Once you're able to process what happened in your past, you may even feel compassion for one's lack of wisdom that led you down the wrong path. Your compassion can provide better understanding for both you and the person(s) who misguided you.

So here we sit with a pile of unhelpful information, a bag of lies, and a mind full of wonder. We are where we are today because of seeds which are thoughts that formed words that power our lives. The seeds that get the most water are the thoughts we believe the most. Those beliefs govern our daily lives. As soon as I began challenging the status quo, I knew almost immediately a lot of bad seeds somehow got planted in my garden. I always had what I thought were grandiose desires that could change the world but for many years I wasn't changing any world and my own world was decaying. Those bad seeds combined with acres of weeds took over preventing a fruitful harvest from growing. The challenge then became to let my garden grow. As any farmer would do, I had to first see my field and make an assessment. I was no longer focused on why my garden had been overtaken but how fast I could clean it up and rip out the weeds so I could then be ready for the next harvest. As a farmer, I knew everything in my garden—good, bad, or ugly—had a root system. A root system that was powered from a seed. The only way to resolve the issue was to find the root. My thoughts were rooted in a seed, and they had to change, which would then, by default, make my life change. So, I had to dig up the root.

Getting to some roots requires more digging. Childhood trauma. Relationships. Heartbreak. Fear. Broken promises. All of these were roots that grew and have been growing since before I was aware of it. Fixing my garden meant I had to flash back. The flashback is a memory that only exists because the root is still alive. Removing the roots kills the entire thought. A thought removed allows for a fresh seed to be planted. Many people remove what they see on the surface layer but never remove what's keeping it alive. They only remove what they can see because it's easier to imagine that it's gone if I brush it out of sight. But like any seed planted, it will grow back stronger every time it's cut.

Fears are roots: beliefs are roots. What is rooted in us will grow out of us. No matter how small it may be. If it's in us and gets enough water, it will grow. Our actions reflect our words, our words reflect our beliefs, our beliefs reflect our thoughts, our thoughts are rooted in the garden of our mind. The life that you imagined is possible if the seeds are planted. If the seeds aren't planted you haven't had the thought, which is fine, but being open to receiving the thought is the first step toward growing your garden. Your garden is your power. It's your strength. It's your passion. It's your purpose.

What you allow to grow and become harvested will either increase or decrease your value. Your mind is the most powerful tool available to you, and it's free of cost. Make healthy deposits into your soil, your mind, which then provides energy to your body and rules your soul. You were born from the seed that already came complete; remove the weeds and chop down the dead and dying trees still standing.

You are the farmer in your life; you reap what you sow. You sow what you believe. What you believe is what you become.

CHAPTER FOURTEEN

Power of a Seed

Looking around we can easily see all the beautiful things that mankind created. We even have the luxury of looking in a mirror and seeing a reflection of ourselves. We can walk outside and take in the sights of plants and trees. These living things sprouted from a seed planted in soil.

Some soil is formed from dirt. Other organisms grow from different kinds of soil, sperm being the soil human beings come from.

Let's go back to the word "seed" again for a moment. One of the greatest seeds a person can cultivate and grow is the seed of a potentially genius idea. All of us at one time or another have heard something that lit a match, that was a catalyst for a new behavior or business idea or change in habit.

In life, it's important to reflect on what we have, where we're going, what we've done, what we've produced, what we've destroyed—all of these things stem from a seed. The right words spoken at the right time will plant a seed inside of us that will grow. The more we believe those words spoken to us, the more that seed will grow into something healthy and thriving.

That seed will begin to form a thought—good or bad, healthy or unhealthy. The initial thought is formed from our perspective and frame of reference based on our upbringing and our DNA. The next thought will be influenced by emotion and the last will be influenced by the perceived future outcome.

The seeds we allow to grow will start to shape us into who we will become. Our belief systems will change. Our identities will start to shift. A growing harvest means a growing individual. The mind must grow for you to produce. We have a seed but we need soil. Often, we like to think of dirt as a bad thing, something you don't want, something viewed as gross or "less than." However, many seeds need dirt to grow. The soil you grow those seeds in will determine the quality of your harvest. How often you water the seed will determine how often and how big it will grow. We are here on this Earth to create and to grow.

Self-reflection is a huge obstacle in the growing process. How do you take a seed, grow it into a harvest, and then share it with the world? It starts with what you already have inside you. You have the seed or seeds. It's now time to figure out whether you need new soil, to fertilize the soil you're already working with, or if you need to water the seeds a little more or a little less.

CHAPTER FIFTEEN

Shattered Glass

What does shattered glass look like? If you touched one of the edges perhaps it would be a little rugged; maybe even cut your skin if you touched it. There are so many pieces all over the place of different sizes and shapes. You can even see your reflection in some of the larger pieces.

What was the glass before it shattered? What shape was it in? How big was it? Was it whole to start with? How did the glass break and shatter everywhere? Does anyone know? I need help because I see broken glass everywhere! When I look out at the world I see shattered glass made of confusion, hopelessness, pride, ego, hurt, pain, love, and joy.

Now it's your turn. Look hard down at that shattered glass and tell me what you see through your eyes. Describe it in as much detail as possible. Paint the picture so I can see it too.

Keep looking. Can you see anything else…maybe a reflection? I can see the reflection. Can you possibly see yourself in that reflection? What if all those pieces scattered everywhere were your thoughts? What if I asked you to put them together again? Would everything align just right? Maybe you didn't like the way it looked to begin with. What image would you like to see when it's complete?

When you are complete what image would you like to see? Take your thoughts and keep the ones you think fit for your life and remove ones that don't. But why did the glass break in the first place? Perhaps what was holding it together wasn't strong enough so it broke. Back to the metaphor, maybe the quality of your thoughts, your thought life, caused the glass to shatter. Maybe there wasn't enough room for some of your thoughts or maybe some of those thoughts should have been avoided altogether.

I know a lot can make its way into our glass, our thoughts, and it gets heavy but you can dump out what you want at any time and recreate. And if the weight of the glass pops you can rebuild it with better structure so it won't break (or if it does it won't break into so many pieces). The idea of wholeness can be your reflection. You are not the shattered glass (sometimes your thoughts will shatter), you are whole. The pieces you need to be you are already there.

Changing metaphors, you're still here because you are the seed. Seeds can be planted anywhere. However, if the soil isn't healthy enough then you can be replanted elsewhere. You are here to multiply. Spread your genius to the world. Show them your heart. Regardless of how many wounds you have, there is still greatness inside you waiting to be experienced by the world.

The only thing shattered is the old you. You have a renewed mind and spirit. You are a beautiful piece of art, a stain glass window—whole and complete.

CHAPTER SIXTEEN

Same but Different

I am a man, I am a woman, I am tall, I am straight, I am black, I am Asian, I am short, I have blue eyes, I have dark skin, I have pale skin, I have big lips, I have a skinny nose. There are so many ways we can describe how we are different. The list can go on and on. What if I told you we were all alike? Man and woman, old and young, black and white—they're all the same thing. What if the only difference in each of us is our belief system?

What we choose to believe with our mind is what we end up seeing with our eyes. Can our eyesight be trusted? When you change the way you look at things the things you look at change.

So, if everything we see is the reflection of our mind then is love our mind? Is peace our mind? Is what I'm taking in producing my reality? Is what I'm seeing and naming things truly what I believe they are? Is my mind describing truth or does it tell a different story that is not based in reality?

What do you see in your mind? What story are you telling yourself? Is that narrative your truth? Is your life all that bad? Or is your perspective about a bad life influenced by the story you're telling yourself? Is life really that hard? Or do you just not like working hard? What if you could work at life and that became your work—life itself became the job, and the place you clock in and out of (your place of employment) was only one part of the overall "job."

Ask yourself, "How am I going be me in this world and produce the beauty in my heart so the world can see it? Whose life am I going to change today? Who am I going lift up above myself so they can know how it feels to win? What else can I do each day to give my heart to the world?

Keep your mind but give your heart away. Can you be love and give love? Can you be hope and have hope? Can you be joyful while having a job? Guess what?! You can be and have anything you want. It's all available for you when you decide it's what you want. You can try out those things you want for yourself as many times as you want. Only you can decide what you will keep and what you will shed.

You were born here as a gift to the world. A promise was made that you would live the life of your dreams. You would never want for anything. You have everything you'll ever need. Your soul is all you need to have all things you've ever wanted. Obtaining your heart's desires will require something new to happen. A new person to be born; a new version of you has to come out. Those characters in those stories inside your head decide who you'll become. They are all pieces of you anyway. Pick one and be it; own it. Become the character you see fit to walk the path of your life. Discover your identity and in that will show you your life's purpose.

Who you are is different from who you were yesterday. You are changing daily by committing to refresh and renew yourself each day. Every day is a new you; you're leaving the old one behind.

So, who or what are you becoming? Love. It's only one thing and it's the only thing.

CHAPTER SEVENTEEN

I Think I'm All That

Who do you think you are? That question often gets asked when someone carries themselves with a sense of confidence. Or when they speak with authority, walks with their head held high, or viscerally steps out on faith.

It's interesting to hear someone say, "you think you're all that." But what should people think about themselves? Should they think they have nothing of value or nothing contribute and act accordingly? No.

How can someone step into the mind of another and tell them what or how to think? Having a strong sense of identity, self-worth, and self-esteem is key to prosperity. Many will challenge this and say that some people are arrogant or cocky. But who are you to be the judge and make that assumption based on your views and perception? What should a confident individual look like? What should fearless look like?

We often lose our identity trying to speak about someone else's identity or experience out of fear that they are something that we aren't. But just because someone has a trait or quality you want for yourself, doesn't mean you've got to break them down. That is never the way to build yourself up.

It's often said you must be humble. Great. Show what a humble person looks like. I'm pretty sure a humble person is just like any other human but we judge who fits that bill based on actions or words spoken. How about you put yourself in the other person's shoes and try to see what they see? You might find that person is humble based on where they came from.

Self-worth is determined by the individual not the ideas or thoughts of others. Over time our identity gets lost or stripped away because the world has its own idea of what confidence is or should be. Confidence can attract fearful people and vice versa. Who are you? Are you confident or fearful? What do you think of yourself and how should another person think of themselves? People (including you) have every right to speak and think highly of themselves. That's not a form of arrogance. It's a form of self-love.

CHAPTER EIGHTEEN

Find a Teacher

Will you listen? Can you submit your ego to another human? What if you don't actually know it all? Would it really hurt to ask for help? Do you have everything you want? Are you where you want to be in life? Getting what you want out of life, following your dreams, or breaking the curse is going to require one to become a student. The school of life has no degrees but fulfills all needs allowing the student to become the best version of themselves.

Since early childhood you are being shaped and taught. What you know is based on the information you retained (or didn't retain) from the wisdom of your teachers. Teachers aren't just the people you encountered in school; they're everyone who has contributed to your life, good or bad because every opportunity, good or bad, is a learning opportunity. As we get older and have more rights and freedom we start to make our own decisions.

We were once told how we should act, shown what's acceptable, and presented with what we can and cannot have. But nobody ever taught us how to get what we want out of life. We were told work at a specific, steady job and that will provide you the life you want to live. We're simply taught a skill, offered a job, and sent on our way. We are running around the world with very little guidance or structure. Because we are adults we can make do, for the most part. But this still doesn't bring us closer to getting what we want out of life.

Life happens so fast and before we know it we find ourselves on autopilot doing the tasks expected of us rather than growing and becoming who and what we want to be. Some of us went the college route so we gained some additional knowledge. For many, college only teaches a specific skill set in regard to work but it doesn't provide us with answers on how to be the person we want to be.

Those who didn't go to college have a different experience, perhaps figuring out life as they go along. Others join the military and the system thinks for you—you just plug in and perform your role or task. You might be fortunate enough to have parents who have grown so much that can still teach you how to operate in life through the ups and downs. Needless to say, many of us haven't had teacher in a long time—someone to sit us down and coach us through life. This is a person who can help us figure out where we are mentally, establish where we hurt, and help us grow us so we can become the person we always knew we were inside. Generation after generation has experienced unresolved hurt in so many ways through systems failing and broken promises. This leaves us wondering what we want and how we go get it. Forget the failed and broken system. It's time for a new paradigm; one where you find at least one teacher who can help you navigate this beautiful and often confusing life.

CHAPTER NINETEEN

Breaking the Curse

Many times we ask ourselves why we are where we are in life. Many of us even question why we do what we do. But at what point do we hold ourselves accountable for the decisions that we've made?

Is there something that you want that you haven't gotten? Ask yourself why you haven't gotten it. We often shift the blame elsewhere—it's because of him or her, because of my mom or dad, or because of my boss. Or we make an excuse as to why we haven't gotten what we want.

However, there's a common denominator in all of this. You. Nobody else is to blame for you not getting what you want. Nobody else is at fault; everything is solely based on how you think and your emotional state. We get exactly what we want in life and out of life.

To get what we want, we have to set out on a journey—one in which we have no idea what will entail. There's going to be some ups and downs along the way and even some trials and tribulations. You may have to overcome some big obstacles well. You'll never know what you'll experience unless you take what many perceive as a risk.

But remember, at one point you told yourself you wanted that thing or experience; you may have even felt you deserved it. Tap into that feeling whenever you pull back or make an excuse as to why you don't have what you want.

If you're going after your goal while doing it your way and like you've always done it, then it's time to start listening to someone else. You are going to have to submit yourself to the wisdom of another human being. By doing this you're not losing any value and you're not less than anything, and you're definitely not less than the person you are learning from. You're simply taking a seat in the classroom of life and you have now become a student listening to the teacher. Leave your pride at the door because there's some wisdom that you can't obtain all on your own. And know and take pride in the fact that someday you'll be the teacher for someone else.

If learning something from someone else still doesn't sit well with you, then it's probably because of your ego and your pride. It's okay that someone else knows more than you, and it's okay that they have something you want. By becoming the student you aren't going to do it exactly their way. You're going to listen to the teacher, see how they did it, and take from them what works for you.

Finding a teacher who you want to learn from is going to cost you something. It could be time or it could be money. What kind of sacrifice are you willing to make to learn so you can get what you want and so you can grow?

In addition to a teacher, you need a strong foundation so you can start moving toward the direction of your desires. If your foundation isn't strong and you can pinpoint where it's weak then you're going to have to go find new soil to build on. New soil is available but everything comes at a price. We often translate price to money but price is anything it takes to get what you want. It's being willing to change your thought life. It's taking time to learn about your fears and then working to overcoming them. This is a price you have to pay. We suffer from a lack of knowledge and often we simply don't obtain knowledge out of fear.

We are so rooted in where we are, we think that taking a step towards what we want would hurt or cause us to be uncomfortable. This goes back to changing your thought life. It's possible to manifest prosperity, happiness, and faith. But again, many of us are so rooted in an unhealthy thought life, we make it near impossible for ourselves to manifest prosperity, happiness, and faith.

The system we live in isn't black or white, man or woman, or a specific race. The system is only your mindset and your beliefs, which then ties into the effort you give toward getting what you want, your discipline, your persistence, and your consistency.

Only you know the life you want to live. Only you have thoughts in your head that determine how you live. You are responsible for the way that you think. What you feed yourself on the inside will pour out of you, good or bad and healthy or unhealthy. The common denominator here is still you.

What is confusing you is fear which then causes anxiety. Patience is required for learning, understanding, growing, and prospering. Patience will allow you to maintain. Patience will allow you to sustain. Patience will allow you to keep pushing forward no matter what happens.

You are everything you need and you have everything you have ever wanted already inside of you. It's time to make your dreams come true and get whatever it is you want in and out of life.

CHAPTER TWENTY

Allow Me to Reintroduce Myself

Who am I? That's a question only you can answer. Not yesterday, or last week, or a few years ago—who are you today? On this journey of life we are constantly evolving and changing. We are changing based on our emotional state, current circumstances, and conscious or subconscious thought patterns.

If you haven't seen someone in a little while, they might comment on how you look different or how tall you are or how you got in shape. But that's just surface level. It's not until we speak that a person knows who they're really talking to.

If you're conquering goals, knocking down fears, or stepping out on faith it will change a person, deeper than what shows on the surface, and will also help that person grow. We often associate pain or conflict as a bad thing but it's simply a teaching moment for us to grow. If a seed never gets water how can it grow? If a seed doesn't have dirt or nutrients, how will it grow? Pain and conflict, much like manure, can be seen as something to avoid. But in reality pain and conflict (again, like manure) are fertile ground for growth and positive sustainable change.

That means "failure" is okay. In order for us to become what we've never been we're going to mess up. We're going to fall. Learning how to stand up in the aftermath is how we grow.

Watering the seed we can now witness a tiny organism, born from nutrients and dirt. Let your seed, whatever that is, grow. Water it, nourish, it, and take care of it. And if you mess up, it's okay. You're learn from it and do better with the next seed or the seed after that.

CHAPTER TWENTY-ONE

You Are Rich

What does it mean to be rich? Is it…

- Money?
- Health?
- Peace?
- Happiness?
- Love?
- Or something else entirely?

Often, when we hear the word rich the first thing that comes to mind is money or wealth. We probably even start to imagine what material wealth looks like, who has it, what it means to you, and where you can find it. You might even start to picture a certain kind of house or a specific kind of luxury car with all the bells and whistles.

But who determines the definition of rich? Ideas about "rich" are tossed around and philosophized over all the time. But in reality, only you know what rich means. You get to define for yourself.

Let's take a step back for a minute and talk about the correlation between money and the word "rich." For many of us we neglect to reflect on the journey we've been on, the obstacles we've overcome, and the mountains we have conquered. The fact that we've survived, have food and water and shelter, have our health, have any sort of peace of mind—these in and of themselves are what makes us rich. To be able to have public transportation, a car, a house, clothes, healthcare—these are things that make many of us super rich.

Growing up in the early 1990s I wouldn't say I came from poverty but I definitely lived in a low income household. Fast forward to today, and in 2020 the world has shifted and the economy has changed in so many ways. What it takes to live costs even more than thirty years ago. The price for so many things cost triple digits—and I'm not even talking about inflation. The cost of goods and services has grown at a much quicker rate than individual or household salaries and income.

As a child you have no money, little to no responsibilities, and you're given everything. As we get older we work at a job and receive a check. The first time you were given any money, that was your first step on the road to becoming rich. Receiving money means you're rich. I know many of us think that rich means millions of dollars but depending on where you came from in life $30,000 might be your million dollars. If you came from a family that had little to no money and you've somehow surpassed your parents' income and provided a life for yourself—that makes you rich. Rich isn't determined by someone else or their journey. It is based on how far you have come. One man's million makes him rich while another man's $50,000 makes him rich.

We often lose sight of how far we've come, comparing our lives to strangers not knowing how far they've come, where they've been, or where they're going. You take someone who was born into millions of dollars and still has the same amount but hasn't accrued any more or any less. They are no richer or poorer than they started off.

Life is sometimes about simply adding a zero or subtracting a zero; something I like to call simple life-math. Items and expectations change based on income and resources. There's always a price which is usually determined by at least one zero and how many zeroes follow the first one.

When we look at quality of life it's not much different in concept for one person or another, but some items require more zeros. This doesn't necessarily make someone richer or poorer—it's simply a discussion of the price it takes to obtain that item.

Material things, which many confuse with enjoying a higher quality of life, are sometimes seen as different form of love. Love is like a double-sided coin. It has two faces. The things we love are sometimes good for us and sometimes they are bad for us. "Love" will then be defined by material wealth or consumption of food, clothes, and fancy things; but truly these are all distractions from looking inward and connecting us with our true source of wealth, which is health and what we've overcome and anything we've ever achieved in life.

One of my sources of wealth or my definition of rich also involves me doing the things I like to do and spending time with the people I want to spend time with. However, if I am surrounded by negative people and I'm not doing what I love but I gain monetary wealth, I'm no longer rich. I get to define what rich means to me. When I'm around happy people I become rich in happiness, but one could also spend time around fearful people and then become rich in fear.

You can become rich in pain, rich in guilt, and even rich in peace. You get to determine what rich is to you. Money is the lowest form of prosperity so being rich in currency doesn't change me. How rich I am mentally will sustain me, make me grow, and help me maintain me in my richest state of being. You have that same ability. Now go out and chase what rich means to you. You deserve it.

CHAPTER TWENTY-TWO

Spoil Your Kids

How many of you have heard phrases like:

- "You should have the world and everything in it."
- "The world is yours."
- "Be the change the world needs to see."
- "You can do all things if you believe."

These are some wonderful sentiments—perhaps even truisms—we tell our kids as they grow up in while fighting obstacles and becoming the person they love. As parents we tend to push a narrative on our kids based on our beliefs due to our upbringing or frame of reference. The wisdom we have is all the wisdom we can give. If we don't know who we are then how can we ever help the young people in our lives find out who they want to become.

As they grow we give and give and give. Are we giving too much or are we not giving enough? By creating the easiest life possible for them is that handicapping them from becoming who they need to be?

As parents or guardians, it's our job to hand off a baton in this race of life. There are no endings, just baton swaps. In track and field when a team member has a baton it's because the runner before them has completed their lap. That means someone was waiting for their chance to takeoff and run. The pace you set determines how much effort you must give to stay in the fight.

Many kids have to pick up a baton; it wasn't exactly passed to them. The exchange during the handoff wasn't smooth. Whatever the circumstances were, the parent sometimes doesn't know how to hand off the baton correctly. They might have been too tired or they may have tossed it because that's what they learned from their parent or guardian. Or maybe their hands were slippery and the baton slipped from their hand. In some cases a parent might not even be in the race and they're watching from the stands.

As a parent it is our job to at least explain to our kids how and why we are where we are in life. But sometimes we don't show them the struggle because we don't have time or we want to protect them from the uglier side of life. If we explain the struggle, we can then facilitate a conversation about how we overcame and let them figure out they, too, can overcome. It's not necessarily our job to teach them a lesson on life as much as it is to show them that life is possible and overcoming is possible too. We are here to hand them a baton and push them forward.

By bringing them in this world we took the lead. They had no say in the matter. We then must run as far as we can as fast as we can so we can then reach great heights, climb mountains, get on the other side where the grass is greener, and then hand them a baton.

Regardless of where you are socially, economically, financially you can still hand off the baton smoothly. This involves wisdom, courage, and faith that your child or children can survive and become one of the greatest individuals to walk this earth. Showering our kids with gifts and material items doesn't mean much if it is going to hurt them. Not teaching them how to keep and maintain the things they've given, and simply acquiring more instead is doing them a huge disservice.

As a parent ask yourself, "what if I could have everything I ever wanted?" Many of you have heard it's not possible but there are people in this world who have proved otherwise. A child has an incredible imagination. They see something they like and want to try to obtain it. Who are we to deny our offspring their hearts desires based on our inability to get them for ourselves? "Spoiling your kids," was a term that was created when we couldn't figure out how to complement someone who was able to get what they wanted for themselves and their kids. Blessed is what is that is called. A child's behavior forms from teaching and understanding that material things are given to them and not to be expected. Spoiled rotten means the fruit has turned bad. How can a good thing turn bad? When it's not properly cared for and loved on poured into and given the proper light. So, don't spoil your kids but bless them instead.

CHAPTER TWENTY-THREE

I Know I'm Beautiful Too

You are beautiful. No, you don't have to thank me for saying it. It's true. You are beautiful. That's what you should be telling yourself. Have you looked in the mirror lately? When was the last time you did and just admired what saw? Because what you're looking at is pretty mind blowing and state of the art.

I know some of you think those things but some of you don't take the time. I don't even need to look at you to tell you that I see the beauty in you too. That might seem weird but it's true. I can see, and more so, feel the beauty inside of you. Whatever you look like, it doesn't matter to me—you are a radiant being and you are glowing.

Look in the mirror today and see what I see. What you're looking at is complete, beautiful, and unbreakable. You are perfect. I know you're perfect because I see my reflection in you. The beam of my inner beauty bouncing from me to you.

So, in case you haven't heard it from anyone today, including yourself… You. Are. Beautiful.

CHAPTER TWENTY-FOUR

Ghostwriter

Have you ever seen a really good TV show or movie; something binge-worthy? And as you're watching the movie you're learning different character's names, where they come from, who they are, or what they like and don't like. As the story begins to unfold you start to wonder what's going to happen next. Will they kill the giant zombie, will they join together and put their egos aside to complete the mission, will the prince win the princess and save the world?

As we're watching the TV show or movie we start to try and relate to the characters we like and root against the ones we dislike based on their actions and reactions. We'll even root for characters who do horrible things, like Walter White on *Breaking Bad*, hoping that they get a second chance.

In these movies and TV shows you have actors, directors, a cameraman, a lighting designer, and many more who are there to bring the story to life. The writer or the writing team may also be on set. This is the person or people who put the story together and who can also change what characters do and say. They put all the plans into motion and then entrust their work to actors, directors, and editors hoping the final product is what they envisioned.

The story you're currently living is your new song and you are the ghostwriter. You are the behind the scenes projecting exactly what you see. The more you keep writing and producing, the better. When you stop writing, somebody else is going to you help you along and show you how. They are also a writer so you can follow along the script they're writing. You help me write mine and I help you write yours. Whatever stories you pay attention to will influence the story you're writing. The dialogue you create inside your head is part of the story as well which is why it's important to always pay attention to the quality of your thoughts.

What are you telling yourself daily? What are you believing and what are you producing? You are the writer so at any given time you can change the story. You can erase it or cover it up or toss it in the air and start from scratch. You are the boss and the writer. Only you are in charge of your story. So what story do you want to tell the world?

CHAPTER TWENTY-FIVE

Stay Focused

Stay focused. I know it's loud inside and outside. Stay focused. I know your attention is being pulled right and left. Stay focused. I know things are on edge right now. But calm down. Stay focused.

It's okay to love where are you at right now; or at the very least you can be content and grateful.

I know other people are doing this thing and that, posting on social media all about the "good life." It's not real. You're doing fine. Stay focused.

Stay present. Stay right here. I know you want to go but just stay here for a moment. Remember when you told anyone or perhaps everyone that this is where you wanted to be? You've waited for so long for this and now you're ready, no itching, to move on. Sit and stay for a moment. Breathe it in. Stay calm. Stay focused.

Eliminate the distractions. What you want and where you're eventually going, it's going to require your full attention. You're so close to the finish line. Remember that every time you make a pitstop on your journey. And when you lose focus, you move further away from your goal.

I know you see so many out having fun and playing but you told yourself you wanted to play to the level of those who are accomplishing great things in life. You wanted to go places and have the energy and stamina to achieve your dreams. To do this you must stay focused.

I know you're going to be everything you want to be. It's almost here. Don't go left or right just keep moving straight, which is the fastest way to travel. Stay focused. You've come too far to stop now.

Stop and play but don't take too long. You've been working so hard and it's okay to take a break from time to time but not at the expense of your goal and your focus. You can still enjoy life while you're on that grind and keeping focused.

Is what you want actually worth it? You told yourself that's what you wanted to do, be, or have. Is it worth the wait if you don't have it? You don't truly know if it's worth the wait. You have to wait until you get it to see how you like it. It can be everything you ever wanted. But you have to be patient. Eliminate distractions. You have to go all in, all out.

If you never had it, you don't know how long it takes to get it. So is it worth it? Only you will know by walking through that door. If you haven't lived the life you wanted, if you're not yet the person you want to be, and it's a matter of walking through that door then why not?

If the life you imagine is what you want then why don't you have it? Does it take long to get the life you want? Is there something you're not seeing because you're being indecisive about what you want? You can see the life you want; you just don't know how to get there. Where do you look first? Who will help you? Do the things you told yourself you can do and needed and wanted. Then seek mentors. But most of all—stay focused.

CHAPTER TWENTY-SIX

You Won't Get Rich at That Price

It's going to cost more than you think. For the kind of value I need will I have to increase cost (the "premium" edition) to get the most out of this product? How else will people know the value of this product? Almost everyone bases value on the price it costs. It could be five thousand or five hundred thousand; there's always a price.

At first you have to see the value in something, the potential, and then you take a leap of faith and make the purchase. You sit with that purchase for a while and then determine whether or not it has increased or decreased in value.

When you see a friend or loved one you tell him whatever experience you had around the value you placed on that product. You may even show or demonstrate the value and then make a recommendation based on the value you put on it. Valuable things will turn a profit and be profitable. Value, in and of itself, is profit.

What makes something valuable to you? Is it tangible items, like things that you can purchase? Is it a word from someone, something spoken? Is it a smile? Maybe it's joy or laughter or courage or faith. The price you place on value is, in a way, a limitation. You're limiting what you would pay for something of value. What price would you put on something that could possibly change your life?

Who do you need to hear it from to believe you can have what you've previously put a limit on? What example do you need to be shown that having this thing of value is possible? What is the price for possibility of a life changing experience? Money doesn't change the experience you have to change the experience. You can go anywhere in the world but what spirit are you going to bring with you? Who are you deciding you're going to be?

Your location doesn't matter because you're going to bring what's inside you everywhere you go. What's on the outside reflects what is on the inside. What's the price for something that reflects you on the inside, which in return, we get to see on the outside. How much did that cost you or how much would it cost? Would you be willing to just take a gamble and spend even a small amount? And what if the amount appeared to be large? Ask yourself why you believe it to be large. Does that number seem unattainable? If so, why?

If you have to spend a seemingly large amount, is it now not worth it? If so, why? You don't know exactly what's inside of it but all you're saying to yourself is that it's too much.

How many other things in life are expensive? Whenever you get where you want to go, will the end experience justify the cost you paid? How much will you have paid to get this knowledge and experience? Was it overpriced? Was it worth it? What is it underpriced? Should it have been free? What if it's all free information but you just refuse to listen? Now you have to pay a price for valuable information that's available every day but for some reason you can't see it or hear it. Would it hurt so badly to listen to examples of good that we can learn from; examples where others felt that at one point the price to go after their goals cost way too much. These are people who we can model parts of our own lives on. People who no longer think about the cost of doing something or going after something they want because they realize the cost is much greater if they don't go after that thing they want.

So, if I met you today who would I meet? How would you describe yourself? What kind of character traits would you use? Would you start off with your career or would you dive in and tell me about all the obstacles you've had to overcome. In life we can either present the journey that we are currently on or we can recite the one that we want to be on or we can even talk about both. It's all possible but only if you allow it. The journey that you're currently on is always better than the past because the past only exists in your memories. Your reality is where you're at today. This story should be the most dominant one. The past should never be greater than your future; it should be a reflection upon your growth. And there's always a new future ready to be birthed inside of you. You must push it out to show the world who you are today. So, what price would you pay to help bring about that new future from within you? Is there a price or is it priceless? Only you can decide, but you must decide. Even if you wait and make no decision, you've still decided.

CHAPTER TWENTY-SEVEN

Clean Up

How did that spot get there? Hmm... That looks like a mess. Let me wipe it up. That's dirty. Let me wash that. I don't like the way it smells—let me deodorize it.

Is there anything in your world you could possibly clean up? Are there places in your life that need to be vacuumed or some windows that need washing? Does the trash need to be dumped? Can you start rearranging some furniture? If you cleaned up what you have what would that look like? If what you currently have is all you will ever have can any of it be cleaned up to look better? Can you see what it looks like in your mind?

What can you do to maximize what you currently have? You may not have everything you want in life but you can take care of the things you do have. That doesn't necessarily mean material possessions or a physical location. You have your health—are you eating properly or do you overeat and supplement your diet with lots of junk food?

You have the gift of speech. Are you silent on important things or do you speak out when you see an injustice?

If we kept the things we have clean, we might not always be looking for the next "great" thing. With great privilege comes great responsibility.

CHAPTER TWENTY-EIGHT

Stockholder

I made a small investment but my return is already tanking. I'm losing stock and my return on investment is no longer the same. I know the stock could shoot back up but today is my only chance. I know this moment is all I have to buy or sell. My overall life experience is reflecting my decision to sell or stay. Where else am I not profiting? What else is draining me and my resources? How much time have I already lost? Stocks are to be sold, kept, and reinvested.

What kind of interest are you expecting on your investments? The mind will control the interest but you devote the time. Where you spend your time reflects the interest you earn based on the investment you made in yourself. It lives inside you. Stock isn't needed if you're the owner of the product (you).

You can't sell something unless you make it available. The thoughts you entertain will decide what you make available and what you keep under wraps. You control every aspect of what you put out in the world because you're the sole owner. When you create, you invest, and when you share that creation you start pulling in shareholders—people who share in that creation with you. You're still the owner but you're granting them access in exchange for something; money, support, love.

Everything we do is an investment. It's up to you whether you're the product owner or a shareholder. Would you rather be in charge or be dictated to? It's your investment—you decide.

CHAPTER TWENTY-NINE

I Would Never Pay That Much

The cost was determined by the creator—the one who invested time and energy to produce the product. It might be too expensive or the price might be too high for you which is perfectly fine. The level at which you want to be in life will indicate the price you're willing to pay. The information they have on that level you want to be at will cost you too. Your whole life was built on a price tag somebody else paid for through time, energy, effort, and sacrifice.

Your understanding of something's value is based on your thoughts which, in turn, reflect the life you live. The things you find valuable you already have. The things that aren't of value or too expensive you simply don't have. What you put value on reflects your thoughts. If money is your value then you put time into having money. If working is of value then you put your time into work. If pain is of value then you put time into pain. Only you determine what is valuable.

So, how much can you afford? How deep are your pockets? How far does your mind go? What are you willing to pay for information or a product? Is it risky? Can you live without it? Do you want to live without it? Only you determine what is valuable to you. As a result you're the one setting the price and paying the cost.

CHAPTER THIRTY

My Metabolism

The metabolism is the process in which your body converts what you eat and drink into energy. During this complex biochemical process, calories in food and beverages are combined with oxygen to release the energy your body needs to function. This energy provides the strength and vitality required for sustained physical or mental activity. Staying healthy requires a good diet. A good diet doesn't limit what I eat—it gives me endless options which then allows me opportunities to try many things.

I eat and drink as much as I allow myself to consume. How much can I really take? Only I know based on how much I've already consumed. My metabolism determines how fast my body is provided with energy. What I put into my body determines how much energy I will have. What I eat will grow inside of me producing energy. My thoughts get fed to me by way of curiosity. The things I think about grow inside my mind producing another kind of energy. A good diet has options. Some diets give you energy to move faster while some diets help you slow down. You have options now because you are on a good diet. You can pick and choose what you will consume so that you can have the most energy to be effective.

Which foods will you consume? Which thoughts will you entertain? Which thoughts bring you energy and which thoughts slow you down? A good diet will give you energy. Your metabolism will break down what you consume converting into good or bad energy. It's based on what you consume both with food and substances and what thoughts you allow into your mind. So, how do you want to feel? What level of energy do you want to exert? How hard do you want to work? What you're taking in determines how hard you have to work based on the amount of energy you give it. At one point you said you'd be willing to work hard. You have to work at your diet and what you consume. The kind of diet you have is endlessly customizable because you have options. You're dreams are endless because you now have a good diet. The life you said you would live is available because you have a healthy diet.

If you don't believe me, then know that breathing is energy. So you always have at least one option.

CHAPTER THIRTY-ONE

Such a Show Off

What do you see? Look in front of you or look inside you. Describe what you see. What's catching your attention? What stands out more than anything? What are your thoughts about the image you see? Is what you believe true about what you see? What information do you have available to assess that image and determine the truth behind it? Your description is based on your belief system.

Who determines the identity of what you see? Tell us. Show us. Be a show off. Your words reflect what's in your mind and is then powered by your actions. All of it starts as a thought. That thought was created based upon what you believe and the identity you gave it. What you give identity to shows in your actions and reactions. What you show us. We can see you because you're such a show off. And that's not a bad thing. You show off all the time; only you know how badly you want to put your emotions on display because you express them through your actions and reactions. That's what we see. That's what we understand about you. Your actions, your propensity to be a show off, is a mirror image of the quality of your thoughts. So, what image do you want us to see?

CHAPTER THIRTY-TWO

Floss Daily

Have you ever made a dentist appointment and while getting your teeth cleaned they flossed your teeth? They took a skinny long cord-like object and ran it in between your teeth. While running the cord in between they can tell if you floss or not depending on whether or not your gums bleed from the cord being so tight.

Have you ever pulled something from between your teeth and smelled it? How did it smell? Your dentist will tell you the food stuck in your teeth for some time can cause bad breath when you speak. It was also cause bacteria to build up in your mouth. If you floss enough your gums won't bleed because when you run floss though it should be very easy to get in and out. Once you finish you then rinse.

Think about your mind using the metaphor of teeth. Is anything stuck in your teeth that is possibly causing damage? Maybe bleeding? Is there anything causing a foul smell? Could you possibly be breathing bad breath in and out and that's what you smell? Which thoughts am I thinking that cause bad breath. What thoughts consume my mind, in effect bleeding me dry? Is anything I'm thinking causing me discomfort. You must loss daily to clean your teeth.

Cleaning our thoughts daily allows for fresh air to come in and out. You "eat" something and it gets stuck. We can't let that happen. Flossing, mental exercises and even physical exercises, help keep thoughts from getting stuck in the mind. The thoughts and beliefs you eat get caught in my mouth when you don't "floss" daily. You know they are caught when they consume your mind. They annoy you. They always hook you back in. You can feel and see it.

Allowing uncomfortable thoughts and holding onto them with a firm grip causes bleeding and discomfort. Consistency in flossing will help ease the pain. So, floss daily to stay fresh and to prevent infection.

CHAPTER THIRTY-THREE

The Shortest Roads Have the Most Lessons

Have you ever tried anything for the first time? You wanted to go somewhere or do something? You were curious about something that brought about excitement. What stands in the way of you doing what you see yourself doing or being?

You see what you want, no? You might not know how to obtain what you want but you can definitely see yourself doing that. That is the equation. You + your thoughts = outcome.

The outcome is what you saw yourself doing. Income is what you felt. It's simple math. There's only one piece in the way of you obtaining what you seek. There's only one "thought" stopping you from solving the equation.

How do you figure out the blank or the missing step to complete the equation? What are next steps in the "unknown?" Have you studied anything and everything around what you want? Have you taken any notes? Have you done any research? Do you know anyone who might have done what you're seeking to do? Did you call them? Have you studied? Have you ever studied only to be taken in the wrong direction? Probably not.

Hearing allows us to imagine. Seeing allows us to obtain.

Have you ever sat with a test and never taken it? Have you ever given yourself an end game and never fully committed to finishing to the end? Have you ever wanted something but never fully committed to getting it so obtaining it is still a mystery? This is likely because you haven't stayed focused long enough to even try and see what can be done to obtain what you want. Committing requires faith because it's going to require time, patience, and understanding while taking yourself through unknowns.

The road traveled toward that thing you want is bumpy but there is a smoother, paved one out there. It involves study, focus, and finding someone who has done what you're looking to do.

You may be thinking you can't financially leave your current situation because you're not sure about this idea working. You're questioning if it will work even though what you're currently doing isn't working. You have already agreed and reasoned with yourself why you "should" take the leap. You know there is something better available for you. Is it just that you haven't decided you really want it for yourself? The idea pops in and out—you now must be ready to commit.

Maybe you've never seen an example of real commitment. You've never seen dedication to oneself let alone a dream or idea that a person could love themselves in such way that they would be love. That's exactly what we are all looking for. A "reflection" of an image of what our mind projects. Every thought is a reflection and we must be careful what we project and then reflect.

If the shortest road has the most lessons then that would mean you are student. You are a coachable. Walking in a straight line, the quickest way to get anywhere, puts you closer to your vision. Be the example of commitment you've never seen before. Then find a mentor who will guide you along the shortest road possible. The path ahead toward what you desire may look scary but that's only because it's the unknown. Keep walking, one foot in front of the other, and pull in a guide, a friend, a coach, from time to time. Ultimately it's you who has to do the work and take the journey. But the only way to take the shortest road is to check in with a guide and feed your mind with food that will provide you with continued focus and commitment.

CHAPTER THIRTY-FOUR

Finding My Identity

You never asked to be here on this planet or what family you would be a part of. You were somehow randomly selected to be a member of a team without knowing what position or role you would play.

You were given a name. However, before you ever had a name, you had a spirit. That spirit came with an identity. You would eventually grow up to like and dislike certain things. You would become shaped by the world around you. You would have parents or guardians who would make sure you didn't grow up like them or who made sure you became just like them.

Soon enough, you would have teachers correcting any kind of behavior that they felt was disruptive or offensive. You'd have friends pushing you in different directions and introducing you to experiences and ideas; some of these you would have seen before and some you only knew existed.

So many factors have contributed to your identity, but more often than not, your identity is a reflection of what others wanted you to be. Yet, there has always been another voice inside of you. Sometimes that voice was loud enough for others to hear, and other times it was so soft that only you could hear it. That voice is your true identity.

Many things you asked for in life, you were told "no," because someone would have you believe that you couldn't afford it or your behavior wasn't sufficient or you that you simply didn't deserve something greater for yourself. You had many bright ideas but were turned down because you were made to believe your ideas were too big or unattainable. Your dreams were killed early in your life by people who couldn't see as far as you could. They couldn't dream as big as the expanse of your imagination.

Generational "curses" were passed down, causing a virus of self-limiting beliefs to infect every family member, which then made its way to you with the potential to limit your future. You were judged for "wrongdoing" when you didn't know any better. You were forced into an environment where you were expected to behave a certain way without truly knowing how to act. For many, at age 18, you were kicked out, thrown to the world, and had to live through a bunch of hard-earned lessons that caused pain instead of blessings. Who am I going to be? What am I going to do? What will I become in this life?

A fresh start is needed. But you still feel like a prisoner of your past. You were taught to hold on so you could remember, when it should have been, "let go so you can learn." Letting go is the start of a fresh, new beginning.

I, Sean, never had a role model growing up. I just had had people I didn't want to be like, so the only thing to be was myself. I had to learn for myself what I liked and didn't like. It was a wild journey. I had to make and own decisions for my life; doing this felt like freedom and power. I had to reestablish who I was so I could understand who and what I would become. My true identity never left me, but as a child and young man, I somehow abandoned it. To reengage with my true identity, I had to unlearn bad habits and toxic traits. This meant I didn't know how to do a lot of things. I embarked upon the unknown. I had no choice but to live by faith. I somehow knew that I could do and be and achieve anything I declared. I am that I am, and there is no other. I could live the life I imagined. I didn't have to stop dreaming. When you stop dreaming you stop believing. I truly believed that I am the god of my life and I could build my kingdom on this Earth.

The world will insist you be like them or work for them… but I had bigger plans. What I was called to do was show the correction of the revelation. You are the blessing that breaks all curses in your life. The blessing is your inheritance. You aren't waiting on god; god is waiting for you. The god in you is waiting to break out of religion and into faith, favor, and prosperity. You have all the power to manifest anything your heart desires, but you will need wisdom to unlock that.

Growing up in poverty once seemed like a curse, but it was actually my lesson for the blessing I've received and will continue to receive. The overflow in my life never would have been possible if I took any other journey besides the one I'm on. Using my stove for heat to now give others warm clothes. Sharing one bathroom with six people to now having too many; I have to hire someone to clean. This proves that renewing your mind, forgiving yourself for what you didn't know, and becoming better by choice is possible if you believe. If you truly believe in the god in you, then nothing can stop you. The life you've always dreamed of is waiting on you.

The lessons shape you so you can handle the blessings. The blessings are meant to be given away so that the glory of the god in you can be seen across the nations. The identity of wealth, happiness, and prosperity was taught as something only a certain kind of person could have. Even when you have these things you're told to hide them because they might offend some people. I'm here as the correction to that kind of thinking.

As a man thinks in his heart, so is he. Let the poor say I am rich. Let the weak say I am strong. Once you declare I AM (similar to Descartes "I think, therefore I am"), you have the power of the god inside activated and ready. The only difference between any human is what they believe the god in them can do or cannot do. What are *you* capable of?

CHAPTER THIRTY-FIVE

Restoring My Identity

If you're like many in this world, then at one point or another, you've given a great deal of thought to who you are and what your purpose is while on this planet. Like me, you may have wondered (or are currently wondering)—*Who am I today?* What do I see when I look at myself in the mirror? Who am I beyond the surface of that reflection looking back at me? What is the quality of the thoughts of that person staring back at me? What I think is exactly what I see. Genesis 1.27 states, "I was made in His likeness and image." I was made In the image of God and so were you. We have been rulers since the day we were born—a king or a queen, bona fide royalty.

My identity from the very beginning was God. I was made in His image so that means I am a piece of Him. "I can do all things in Christ that strengthens me," Philippians 4:13. I am the ruler over my body and mind. My mind controls the quality of my existence. Where I believe I am is exactly where I'll be. If I believe that I am at peace then the statement is true. If I believe myself to be in hell, then that statement is true as well.

The identity thief has robbed many of a happy and fulfilling life that all of us deserve.

The creation of human life starts as a seed. The baby has an identity before it has a name. The name is presented as a label to help distinguish one person from another. For many, we were given a label and then instructions on how to be that label before we ever understood our identity or that self-identity even existed.

At some point, the world shifted from allowing for self-discovery to labeling people and expecting them to adhere to that label.

How do I find my identity? You may ask. You have begun your quest in the wrong manner. You have an identity already, what's inside. You simply need to restore, to return to factory settings before someone else gave you a label that isn't entirely you. This may seem impossible because you currently recognize what you know, see, and have through the lens of your current "identity." But this idea of identity is a fantasy; an imaginary thing that exists in your mind. It's not real because it's someone else's perceptions and world view projected onto you.

Whatever identity you want, the one that already exists inside you, the truest form of you, will come to light if you speak it aloud and then follow the direction it leads you in. This isn't the direction someone else determined was right for you and your life, but a direction based on your truest self. You can cross out that old label and replace it with one that connects with the real you inside. What's inside isn't a label but your identity.

Your entire life will now be projected through this identity—the subject matter you study, who you become friends with, and the quality of your relationships, your relationship with self, and more.

You now get to be whoever you want to be; whoever you claim to be. If you want to be beautiful and wealthy (the word has a lot of meanings) and purposeful and kind—and speak those desires aloud on a consistent basis—then that is exactly the direction your life will take. You will constantly be working on yourself and to bring to the forefront those qualities, attributes, and actions you wish to see in your life. "I think, therefore I am," the old saying goes.

The vision of your life will start to come full circle. Everything you envision will become part of your reality. If you are love and envision it, then love is what you will become. The same goes with peace and wisdom and understanding and anything else. Your job will change. Your relationships will change. Take back your identity; don't be what others have labeled you or what others expect of you. Work toward connecting to your truest self by taking the time to state with conviction that which you wish to be and receive; do so consistently and watch the quality of your life change for the better.

CHAPTER THIRTY-SIX

Hire a Trainer

When working out sometimes people hire a trainer to help teach them how to transform their body or to correct them when they aren't working out efficiently or properly.

Along the same lines, a sports coach will look for the best talent but beyond that, he or she will look for coachable players. This is someone who can be corrected, taught, and be able to have the greatness inside of them coaxed out, then molded and refined.

In life due to the build-up of pride, ego, and fear one may find it difficult to take constructive criticism; the kind that a coach or trainer provide. Often constructive criticism is seen as offensive or attacking. Our ability to be corrected—to be trained or to be coachable—is the only way we can change. If I want X but I'm not getting it, then I have to make a change. If I can't see that I'm even not getting close to achieving X with my current actions, then I might need some correction; someone to point me in the right direction.

The more you keep an open mind to new information and change, the more you'll allow constructive criticism in your life; ultimately making for a smoother process to get whatever it is that you want or need.

Nothing in life ever changes by itself. What changes is your perspective. Sometimes the only way to change your perspective is to be "coachable" or to hire a personal trainer for your life.

CHAPTER THIRTY-SEVEN

Rent Free

What is the quality of your thoughts? Are they positive or negative? What do you choose to focus on? The time you spend thinking about anything allows you to see the importance or value you place upon it. Is what you're thinking about costing you money, time, peace, or, joy? Are your thoughts paying you what they are worth? What kinds of thoughts are living rent free inside of your mind costing you the most precious commodity you have? Time.

CHAPTER THIRTY-EIGHT

My Script

If you're in my life it's because I chose you for you to be there. I wrote the script of my life to have you in it. The story of someone's life is not a script with multiple writers—you and you alone write the script of your life.

People are a part of your script and stay as long as you think of them. You control every aspect of your life—what you think, what you do, and who you allow in it.

If you don't like how your script is unfolding then there's a problem and it needs fixing. If you like the way your script is turning out, then that's great. Either way, only you determine the quality of your script and what stays and what goes.

You are the only one who controls your thoughts. Any new script revisions you get from someone else must be reviewed and processed in your mind. But only you determine what to do next—incorporate the revisions or toss them aside. It's all based on what you want. What you want is determined, in part, by what you allow because what you allow is what will continue.

CHAPTER THIRTY-NINE

My People Don't Support Me

Are you still looking for support from your peers, family, and friends? Are you still desperately trying to get them to see what you see? To invest in your vision?

The moment you grow mentally you are no longer on the level you once were. The elevation of your mind shifted you into a new dimension. Often, people are afraid of what they aren't, what they don't know, and anything new. The new you may be hard to understand and even threatening to them (because of their lack of understanding).

If the person is worth keeping in your life, then have a little patience with them. On the other hand, new heights require new people. These new people should have a similar ethos or vibration as you. People who will understand you and vice versa. These new people will likely relate well to you and be able to see your vision.

The support you need and are looking for is largely not in what you left but in where you're going. Most people behind you don't have the capacity to support you and that's okay. People in front of you will support your mission, in part because they too have embarked on a similar journey and needed the support they're now providing you.

CHAPTER FORTY

I Never Knew I Wasn't Rich

Who told you something was wrong? Who told you that you didn't have enough? Who told you that you were less than? Who said you were broke? Who even defined the word "rich?"

There was a moment in time when you had no understanding of what it meant to be without. You never knew anything was wrong until someone told you. Everyone is rich. The level of their wealth is based solely on their understanding and belief system. Some identify rich with money. Money is obtainable and has a certain value to purchase things. Once you make a purchase then the item in place of the money represents value or wealth.

But money only has worth when you make a purchase or give it away. Otherwise, it has no value. By placing improper value on money (calling it "rich" or "wealth") society often makes a judgment on a person's value based on how much or how little money they have. But a person can be no better or worse based on the amount of money in their bank account—it is what it is. My own wealth should not be measured by what someone else does or doesn't have.

Therefore it's up to you and only you to define your version of what being rich or wealthy means. If you want an identity that involves being rich, then how do you define it? Rich in friends, in charitable giving, in leisure time, in children, in teachable moments? Money doesn't make me, you, or anyone else rich. It's up to each of us to define the word "rich" and then take the appropriate actions every day to live out our ideas of being wealthy.

CHAPTER FORTY-ONE

Wounds to Wisdom

For each of us, there are things we want that we didn't receive. There are things we receive that we didn't want. There are things that happen that you understand while there are other events and circumstances that you don't understand. They are things you can control and other things out of your control.

Many of us have been let down, hurt, or disappointed. Some of the hurt and pain have left emotional scars. Clearly, you don't ever want to feel any of that pain ever again. Fortunately, you no longer have to be stuck in it because it's no longer happening. But sometimes the pain returns when thoughts of those experiences arise.

Often, we don't know why the thing that caused us pain happened. We can wish it never happened but it did and here we are today. Your presence in this moment means you have overcome. The painful thing didn't kill you because you were strong enough to survive. Your willpower was bigger than the painful thing, and you didn't even know how great your willpower was until you were tested.

It may look as if the world is defeating us because of our current circumstances. It may appear as if we're not winning because society often points to someone and says they're "a winner" and you don't believe you look or sound like that kind of person. You may have even determined you aren't a winner.

Life becomes complicated when you start mislabeling things and then telling yourself what you can and cannot have and what you are and are not based on those erroneous labels. These labels, unfortunately, become part of your identity. This identity was created by other people because they don't know you who are at your core nor do they know themselves. A great deal of people give power to their false identity and let it rule over their lives.

Forget the identity someone else gave you. If you're having a hard time connecting to your truest self, go back to your wounds. The obstacles you've overcome in your life will tell a great deal about who you are, and perhaps even where you can go in the future. There is a great deal of wisdom from the scars you bear.

CHAPTER FORTY-TWO

The Way You Think is Based Upon a Teaching

At some point in life, someone taught you about emotions and it was likely they didn't have a conversation with you about it. They taught you by example, and often the teacher is not in touch with their emotions to be a healthy example. Now you're feeling an emotion but you don't know what to think about it or how to process it. You may not even know that emotion's true name. It may feel scary or even paralyzing.

In this case, listen to your gut because your gut doesn't process thoughts (and yes, it processes thoughts) much differently than the mind. Your mind processes emotions based on a belief system that has been built over the course of decades, whereas your gut processes emotions based on millennia of the evolution and revolution of our ancestors.

Your mind has been programmed based on your environment. You've been hurt for so long and you've healed because your mind helped the process, but it didn't come with any wisdom because your mind is based on that faulty belief system. The healing wasn't intentional but was more reactionary. You haven't developed any kind of discipline for your life so that unhealthy patterns or susceptibility to running into certain difficult patterns don't continue to repeat. When there is no intention and the mind takes over, the emotion you're feeling is likely anxiousness due to uncertainty that the past will come back to haunt you. Those thoughts may then spiral out of control.

If you want more control over your thoughts, your anxiousness, your emotions, and your mind; then you must first go back to your gut. What is it telling you? If you don't know how to interpret your gut (aka your intuition) then find a teacher. Who do you know who is in touch with their emotions? What kinds of books or blogs or radio shows or podcasts can you consume to teach you more about your gut, emotions, and mind?

If you want to start a family you wouldn't seek out examples of people who don't have a family. If you $10 million, you wouldn't seek out advice on what to do with it from someone who spends money frivolously or who doesn't have a bank account. If you want to heal you can't glean advice from people who are still hurting and making no effort at healing. If you want something new you have to stop doing old things and try something new.

A good teacher will take you to places you've never even dreamed. A good teacher will show you how to end repetitive cycles (for example, trauma, abuse, entering unhealthy relationships) by uncovering the patterns in your thoughts and behavior that led you to the place you're currently in.

Come back to your gut, put away the old patterns, and seek out teachers as if your life depends on it (it does).

CHAPTER FORTY-THREE

Helpful Truths

Make up your mind that you can't turn back because you've already wasted too much time not being your truest self.

You can't keep telling people you're lonely if you don't know how to be by yourself as your own best friend. Your constant attachment to others does not come from a healthy place. What is it inside of you that you're trying to avoid?

Nobody completes anybody else. You complete you based upon your knowledge and wisdom you currently possess.

You are a master. You've climbed walls you thought were unscalable and developed scars from events you once thought you'd never heal from. You are a master at persevering. You are a master at overcoming. You are a master at believing that it will get better.

The strongest fighters are the ones with the most wins but with the most fights.

All of the pain we've experienced was wisdom in disguise.

If I want something in life, I need to be around people who are achieving that same thing. You attract what you are. That's often why people who agree with you are very similar to you.

We know exactly what you stand for based on the crowd of people you're preaching to.

Life isn't going to change because you speak differently; life will change when you become what you talk about. You have to become what you want to be.

The reflection of what you are shows. Your spirit has a face and a voice.

The sooner you change the sooner you'll see what you attract.

Restoring your identity is key to success. Your identity will pay you. Your identity will honor you. Your identity will reflect exactly who you are, what you've become, what you've overcome, and what you're currently doing.

The journey toward finding our purpose in life starts with not knowing. The only way to begin moving is by having a bit of faith. You had an idea or a dream about your life's purpose. Now you need faith that the direction you're walking in will bring about the vision you have for yourself.

Living by faith would seem impossible until it has been done. Faith brings action, which is the only way you're able to see what comes next. As you embark upon your journey, you may not see huge amounts of progress. However, as you go through the trial and error process, you are actively becoming the vision that was once only in your head.

Success isn't defined by the achievement but by the fact that you had faith and tried. Who were you when you started the journey and who have you become along the way?

Life will change for you once you're able to live carefree from the expectations of the world around you. Growth will occur once you're solely invested in the promise you made to yourself to stop allowing things into your life that hinder your potential.

You are the "voice" or the subconscious echoing inside your head.

At one point in your life, where you are now seemed impossible to get to. You couldn't imagine what this experience could look like because you had not yet tried to step toward it. Each time you thought about it you got closer. Each time you stopped thinking about it you pushed you further away. You are your thoughts. If you can't even envision it, or won't try, then how can you have the thing you think you want or need?

Whenever you make a promise to yourself, you must keep that promise top of mind; in front of you at all times. You see nothing else but that promise.

When I see clearly my thinking adjusts to anticipate where I'm going. This requires me to listen more and speak less.

I only know how long I was in hell when I decided I no longer wanted to stay there.

The quickest way to get anywhere is in a straight line.

Whenever I tell myself I have more time, I go slower. The less time that I perceive to have the faster I go.

What you have time for has time for you.

What you don't have time for never happens.

What is living rent-free inside your mind that's not paying you in return?

The money I make is the money I'm worth, but I'm only worth what I invest in, and what I invest in is what I deemed important.

What I allow is what I'm okay with.

If I want to connect with someone, they will never hear me until I learn to speak their language.

Your wildest dreams are the furthest you can go in life, so dream big.

What I do is what I have time for. What's important is what I show up for. What I show up for I want to be a part of. If I'm a part then I'm now connected. Once connected now I have power. Once there's power I have energy. Energy determines performance.

What I have is what I wanted. What I wanted is what I got. What I got is what I paid for. What I paid for cost something. What cost me was time.

Time is happening now, today. Today, the present moment, is all we have.

CHAPTER FORTY-FOUR

Identity Restored

Who am I? Many respond with their name and I understand why that would be a person's first reaction. Your given (or chosen) name is meant to represent who you are and how the world identifies you. But before you had a name you were only DNA. You were born complete and whole.

DNA, on a metaphorical level, is what you're made of. So who are you? What are the thoughts you think about yourself that confirms, for better or for worse, what you are?

As an African American male under the age of thirty, there is a narrative that exists in the world that because of slavery you have been at a disadvantage. Because of what happened to your ancestors you now pay the price and have to start at the bottom. Because of the color of your skin your road traveled will be more difficult. The white man Is after you and stopping you at every turn. The system isn't built for people like you. I once believed that narrative, but I discovered it wasn't true; at least not for me.

Buying into a status quo belief system will either keep you from doing something or keep you believing you can have something. Those beliefs might even cause you to do something harmful or careless. The life that others breathed into these words, these status quo belief systems, are not and never were your own words. These words came from someone, who like many, is not in touch with their identity. So how could they be in touch with your thoughts, belief systems, life trajectory, and identity?

What you are, what you can be, and what you can achieve all *seem* to be laid out in advance. It appears to be influenced by the things that make us different—black/white, young/old, tall/short. But what separated humanity wasn't the white person, the tall person, or the blind person. We became separate when we started to view the outward differences as something to fear rather than celebrate. Yet, Genesis 1:27 says we were created in the image of god.

Sadly, we as a species took on the identity and a spirit of something less than what we were made to be. Our existence soon revolved around fighting ourselves and others to get back whatever we felt was taken from us. Give me back what I know is mine—my heart, my land, my money, my time, my dignity.

Tangibly speaking, a person can have all those things taken from them, but no one can ever take away your identity; your truest self. Who you say you are is what you become. What you become is what you do. What you do determines your strength, which then determines how much weight you can carry. You are capable of so much more than you even realize. You were born complete and whole. You are a chosen people. You were made to inherit wealth, love, happiness, and peace—ask and you shall receive.

Connecting with your true identity uncovers your purpose. Your purpose is the reason you're on planet Earth. Restore your identity to show the world and yourself the greatness that lives within you.

CHAPTER FORTY-FIVE

God

The day I became god was a normal day, just like the many that had preceded it. That particular day I spent thinking about who I could help if I helped myself first. I read as I would often do, about all the great inventors. I didn't care much about their fame or income, but how were they able to build something that helped so many people.

Over the years, I've been a self-made entrepreneur opening several successful businesses—yet I knew that no matter how successful those businesses were, I still had not opened the right one. I'm a young, Black male with no college degrees who went from poverty to opening multiple businesses and winning major awards all before the age of 30. But all of that wasn't good enough…because, to me, it wasn't all that difficult.

I read and heard a lot of the stories about business ownership—it's not easy, be prepared to lose money, most businesses close within the first year—but many of those I found were not my truths. Big faith, determination, and focus will get you pretty far along with some hard-earned wisdom.

I could drive past my business location, look at my sales, look at my life, and it would seem like I'm living the American dream. But in reality, I've always known I was destined for something more, something greater; I was getting warmer but I was not "there" quite yet. I had to keep pushing… but in what direction? I had a life that on paper made sense but it still wasn't clear to me. In late 2019, a virus was rumored to be causing numerous deaths and by early 2020 it was called the deadliest virus ever. The world shut down, putting almost everyone on lockdown. Everything closed; businesses were shut down. The world feared it was the end of human life. For many years, I lived in what I called the real world. Death happened and is happening every day. Nothing is guaranteed, and life is what you make it. As I watched the world panic, people losing lives, people losing jobs, I felt very much at ease. Everything in my life seemed pretty normal. As an entrepreneur in my daily life, my focus was if you didn't make money you didn't eat. If you don't make money, you had to no home. If you didn't pay your bills, they would kick you out. What the world was experiencing psychologically for the first time was something that so many had to deal with every day of their lives. Not eating and homelessness was now a real possibility, and an adjustment was needed.

During the pandemic, I didn't have to, but I closed two of my businesses. The virus had no effect on my decision; it was just timing for the season of revelation that I was in. I worked around the clock for years, but the one thing I knew I was losing, regardless of money, was time. The time I spent building and working took me away from places I needed to be building elsewhere. The opportunity presented itself to move on, so in doing so I was okay. I needed to switch gears and define "success" in a whole new way.

I understood where's there's a gap there's opportunity but vision is required to see where you should go in life. I always wanted to help people, but I knew anything I ever did I only did for myself, and people benefited from it as a byproduct. So, I said I would start writing about my journey. I knew growing up I didn't read much and the culture I'm from not many read at all, so I felt that was a good place to fill a gap. I would often read business development books but none of them spoke to me in words that I fully understood. I knew I needed to read something direct and impactful, but basic enough for me and for others to understand. So, I wrote three books that talked about a revelation I had regarding what I once thought to be right, how I never knew other alternatives, all of which ultimately changed my life.

In my second book, *The Power of a Seed*, I broke down how seeds which are thoughts have built our lives. The wrong seeds when watered will grow into corruption of the mind and heartache. Seeds of love when watered will produce peace, happiness, and growth. Weeds will grow trying to destroy a fruitful harvest. Our minds are a garden and seeds are the thoughts. After the harvest, one must till the soil ripping everything out, so when a new season arrives (and our lives are always full of new seasons), the right seeds can be planted to grow a harvest of overflow.

My third book, *Restoring My Identity*, walks you through how a clean start can happen whenever you're ready to move forward. Looking down causes you to erroneously see how far you *can't* go while looking up shows you how high you can be.

This year, 2020, presented a great deal of knowledge and wisdom to me. A curse was on the world. In 2020, a virus caused people to lose their identity, and fear set in. New beliefs were formed. Faith lost its way.

People around the world lost sight of their identity and the fact that god lives inside each of us. They asked things like *If there was a god, why would he do this? If there was a god, why can't he stop this? If there was a god, why is he not showing up?* Unhealthy seeds were planted and watered daily by the news and word of mouth making almost a year of tremendous difficulty feel like decades of torment. Unity and faith was and is needed to get things back to normal; to a place of health and wellness for all.

The truth about how people felt began to surface; much of it rooted in fear and distrust and disconnected from their truest self. We all wanted the same thing—safety, truth, freedom, love, connection, prosperity—but we viewed how to obtain these things in different ways. Those who operated from a place of scarcity pointed to others or groups of people to be at fault for the state of the world. Those who came from a place of abundance gave of their time and resources and decided a change was first needed from within before others could be blamed. The only person you have control over is yourself. The only person who can control you is you. Accepting full responsibility for self is how we move forward. Secondly, we forgive ourselves, for we have all sinned. Religious or not you have done bad things or had bad thoughts at some point. We must stop making excuses for why we are so different and then judging others for whatever they did that's so much worse than your transgressions.

We must unlearn all the toxic traits we have developed over the years. This happens by making knowledge available for everyone. We must also become students. Wisdom is the only way to grow. When you stop learning you've stopped growing. We must also plan to work and work the plan. Start believing in yourself. You are confident, smart, strong, and beautiful. You were made perfect, and that includes factoring in your imperfections. Ask questions until you understand what you're doing. It doesn't matter how long it takes; as long as at some point you're understanding. Your pace is fine—you're only running you're own race and no one else's. Find the capacity to be excited about your life. Life is precious. Be happy for the place you're in and even more excited by the place you're going. The energy you need to move forward is all mental. And you will need energy to enjoy life. Don't finally get what you want and then be too tired to enjoy it. Develop a routine—you will need to develop discipline and accountability. You need a routine; not just in the places you go or the things you do, but most importantly the words that you speak and think. Smile and greet people. Offer a compliment to what and who you like. Start dreaming again. Your imagination is your future. Make your wildest dreams last forever by building them in such a manner that they never go away. Keep the faith. Faith is the evidence of things hoped for and the conviction of things not seen. Once you form a thought, you make the declaration that it's yours. Hold onto those dreams because that's the vision you are ultimately making your reality. You can't possess anything physically that you haven't received mentally. The rich life you imagined is inside of you. The life you want isn't a dream; it's inside of you waiting to get out. You are the key that unlocks all of your miracles.

You have God-given power to rule your life. You have to build it brick by brick. Thought by thought. Seed by seed. It's getting started that stops most people. You only get one life to live. When will you start to make it the way you want it? When will you stop watching and start doing? When will you stop talking and start listening? When you will stop procrastinating and start writing? When will you stop arguing and start building? When will you do all the things you expect others to do? You are the god in and of your life. Anything you want, you can create. Anything you think you can have. Start praying to yourself for yourself to develop better habits. Hold yourself accountable, not hostage. You know your issues. They are only issues because they don't bring you peace. Thoughts are the difference between happy and sad. Train the positive thoughts more than you train the negative. That means your words matter and the thoughts you think matter. How you see yourself and view others matters. Your language will change when your thoughts change; your life will change once your language changes.

Growing up, I often heard, "Sean, you talk white." It wasn't until recently when I realized I wasn't talking white; I was talking right. Speaking clearly so I could be heard. Using phrases that spoke to where I was mentally. I was using better words that carried more weight effectively instead of using poor words that proved my immaturity and revealed my negative emotions. My identity was taught to me through my skin color and justified with my condition reflecting my position as something less than everything else. For decades, this culture developed certain mindsets but without any context.

- Be thankful for what you have.
- If God is going to bless you, then He will.
- Respect elders because they are right.
- Stay in a child's place.
- Once you get a good job, keep it.
- It's hard out here for Black folks.
- You have to be famous to live like them.

- Everybody can't be rich.
- Men should do a laborer's job because they are strong.
- Work overtime to make more money.
- Join the military if you want a better life.
- Your oldest sibling is entitled because they are older.
- Pain makes you strong.
- If it's one thing, it's another.

So many erroneous and unhealthy thoughts ruin the human mind because of people who never knew something greater. They couldn't see greater or how to obtain greater so all they know is everything they believe you can have. They didn't realize you can be thankful but still want more because you still don't have what you want. They never understood if god is going to do it, that meant the god inside of you was going to have, think, and believe achieve what you wanted so you can get ever closer to your best self. We were made in His image. The god in you is the god of hope and glory. I and the Father are one, and I can do all things through Christ who strengthens me.

You are the god they speak of. I am the god they speak of. You no longer get to tell me what you think is best for me. It's not your life. I have desires and wants that you don't. Your skin color does making living any harder than what the next person has to deal with. Regardless of your skin color, it's going to be hard getting what you want. It's going to be hard not having what you want. You have to decide that I AM and remain that. Stories of success are all the same. Starting at the bottom isn't a disadvantage; it is the beginning. Your very own Genesis.

There is only one of you. How will make sure you are remembered after you're gone? What will you do that is great in order to change your life and the lives of others? How far will you go? The toughest battle involves believing you won't stop until finish the race. The lessons along the way are mandatory so when you receive the blessing you can sustain the blessing.

Everyone's road will look different, but the glory is the same. The light shines brighter the closer you get to it. When you want more you have to grow more. Gaining more faith and greater knowledge. Student first, master second. They have the same thing you can have if you believe how they believe and if you work how they work—but most importantly if you have the mind of god. The mind of royalty. The mind of a ruler. The mind of a lover. The mind of a friend. The mind of forgiveness. The mind for understanding. The grace for correction so you can get realigned to walk in authority. You are what you think and what you think you say aloud.

Think like a god. Honor like a god. Serve like a god. Speak like a god. Reaching the top creates a new bottom. You have now risen above what you once were. You have reached a place where you're metaphorically walking on water; doing what once seemed impossible. Who could have imagined? You could because that's how you got to where you are now. Your imagination is your tour guide to the life you want and the life that you can have. Start dreaming again. Childlike faith means you can have anything in the world. Adult-like wisdom teaches you how to receive the world you deserve (and you deserve the best).

Made in the USA
Coppell, TX
24 August 2021

61076830R00108